D0866968

FOUNTAIN HOUSE

FOUNTAIN HOUSE

Creating Community
in Mental Health Practice

ALAN DOYLE,
JULIUS LANOIL,
AND KENNETH J. DUDEK

COLUMBIA UNIVERSITY PRESS
NEW YORK

Columbia University Press
Publishers Since 1893
New York   Chichester, West Sussex
cup.columbia.edu
Copyright © 2013 Alan Doyle, Julius Lanoil, and Kenneth Dudek
All rights reserved

The authors are donating all proceeds generated by the sale of this book to Fountain
House, New York, to further its mission of hope and empowerment to people
everywhere who are living with mental illness.

Library of Congress Cataloging-in-Publication Data
Doyle, Alan.
Fountain House : creating community in mental health practice / Alan
Doyle, Julius Lanoil, Kenneth J. Dudek.
   pages cm
Includes bibliographical references and index.
ISBN 978-0-231-15710-0 (cloth : alk. paper)—ISBN 978-0-231-53599-1 (e-book)
   1. Mentally ill—Institutional care—United States—History.   2. Mentally ill—New
York (State)—New York—Rehabilitation.   3. Mentally ill—Deinstitutionalization—
New York (State)—New York.   4. Community mental health services—New York
(State)—New York—History.   5. Fountain House (New York, N. Y.)   I. Lanoil,
Julius.   II. Dudek, Kenneth J.   III. Title.
   RC439.55.D69 2013
   362.2'2097471—dc23

                                                                    2013010188

Columbia University Press books are printed on permanent and durable
acid-free paper.
This book is printed on paper with recycled content.
Printed in the United States of America
c 10 9 8 7 6 5 4 3

COVER DESIGN: Christopher Sergio

References to websites (URLs) were accurate at the time of writing. Neither the
author nor Columbia University Press is responsible for URLs that may have expired
or changed since the manuscript was prepared.

This book is dedicated to the memory of
John Henderson Beard (1923–1982),
whose unique insight and fierce determination
created Fountain House and its hope for recovery
for anyone afflicted with mental illness.

CONTENTS

CONTENTS

FOREWORD

This book on the origins and stance of Fountain House is likely to become a classic. It illuminates the driving ideas behind one of the major movements in mental health care and advocacy. Although focused mainly on the original Fountain House in New York City, it portrays the source of what is now a global movement. I anticipate that it will be widely read and discussed. It could (and should) have a significant influence on future developments in mental health.

One of the remarkable features of the book is that the authors find ways to express profound ideas in language that is clear and engaging. What they have written will be accessible and informative for a wide range of readers. The book is also scholarly and will be essential reading for those who are interested in the history of consumer and advocacy movements as well as that of mental health care. The material is novel, in that the story of Fountain House has not been told before in parallel with the evolution of the thinking behind it. That it has origins in the New York settlement houses established for poor and immigrant communities in the early twentieth century will be surprising to many.

When I read the book, I found it particularly compelling that the basic principles on which Fountain House was established were so clearly distilled even in its early days. This clarity is exemplified by the principle of "the need to be needed." As the book explains, a fundamental premise of Fountain House is that we all "need to be needed." This is a principle that is understandable to everyone. The simplicity of the phrase should not deceive one into thinking that the concept is obvious or easy to apply. It is by no means obvious, as evidenced by the fact that what we generally encounter instead are mental health services that do not use this premise to inform their practices. Indeed, when the originators of Fountain House adopted this premise as the basis for building an environment to promote recovery from mental illness, it represented a profound insight. The perseverance required to find ways to effectively apply this principle, which was done by establishing a "working community," is elaborated throughout the book.

One reason for emphasizing this point is that sustainable changes in community mental health care require strategies that are based on premises that can be simply communicated and understood. These premises need to be understood not only by advocates or practitioners, but also by users, informal caregivers, service providers, community groups, government agencies, and other constituencies, many of which are not primarily focused on mental health. From a global perspective, one has to assume that some constituencies will have only basic or no literacy. Sustainability requires at least that these constituencies will not sabotage the movement for change, and at best that they will be active supporters. The history of community mental health is replete with approaches that were initially well developed but not widely taken up or sustained. Among the many reasons, an important one is that often the underlying rationale for these approaches was not widely appreciated and was not articulated in terms of something that all human beings require and can understand. Another is that the approaches were not sufficiently adapted for use across vastly different local contexts. Both sustainability and meaningful adaptation of specific practices depend upon readily communicable basic ideas as a starting point.

I believe this book will be useful to anyone interested in mental health, in any country. Indeed, the principles that underlie Fountain House are particularly relevant today in low- and middle-income countries. The actual uptake of the book in these countries will be contingent on the ability to see that the basic premises of Fountain House are adaptable to a variety of very different contexts. The distillation of these premises into universally understandable principles, however, creates the potential for this uptake and adaptation to occur.

EZRA S. SUSSER

INTRODUCTION

Fountain House is about an idea in [psychiatric recovery] whose time has come. Most people who know of Fountain House think of it as a place for people with psychiatric illnesses located on West 47th Street in New York City's historic Hell's Kitchen neighborhood. They associate its founding in 1948 with a group of ex-patients and their wealthy sponsors amid high hopes of helping one another to reenter society upon their discharge from a mental hospital. They may even be aware of the formative influence of John Beard, who labored for more than twenty-five years on the early design and development of Fountain House. Most are unaware, however, that Fountain House is more than an operational endeavor that achieves recuperative results with its membership. It is an idea whose expression combines both a compelling ideal of human nature, i.e., community, and a treatment methodology, social practice, that has inspired its replication in hundreds of places throughout the world.

Some would contend that Fountain House, while a pioneer for those living with mental illness in the past, represents a practice that is old and outmoded (Whitley, Strickler, & Drake, 2011). They claim that it has lost its relevance as a contemporary concept of recovery in mental health policy and practice (a proposition that this book challenges). The recovery paradigm (Anthony, 1993; Hogan, 1994; Whitley & Drake, 2010) holds out the hope of recovery for those who live with an illness that was once considered to be chronic and progressively debilitating. The paradigm affirms that they can live active, productive, and assimilated lives in society and asserts the rights of people with serious mental illness for self-determination and control over the treatment of their illness. Consequently, any topical discussion of broad-scale public policy for improving mental health services must integrate consumers of mental health services as active participants in their own recovery and be able to demonstrate the outcomes of personal empowerment and social inclusion with tangible evidence (hence, the call for evidence-based practice).

In point of fact, Fountain House, as we shall describe here, established all of these ideas and practices as essential to recovery and the social inclusion of people with mental illness decades before their broader public recognition in the 1990s. Long before these ideas became accepted practice in rehabilitation, Fountain House had charted the basic coordinates of employment and housing for people with mental illness, as well as other current practices in mental health (Sowbel & Starnes, 2006). Through decades of reflective trial and error Fountain House has forged a robust model, which in 2011 was recognized by the U.S. Substance Abuse and Mental Health Services Administration (SAMHSA) as replicable and was placed on the National Registry of Evidence-Based Programs and Practices (http://www.nrepp.samhsa .gov/viewIntervention.aspx?id=189).[1] In *Fountain House*, we explicate how the values of hope, empowerment, evidence-based outcomes, and social integration are translated into practice and how our idea of a *working community* speaks directly to the needs of today's broken mental health system.

Deinstitutionalization and Recovery

We believe that the present mental health service delivery system in the United States is in need of repair. We see it firsthand every day in the lives of our members, who without adequate community support services are left completely to their own devices. Under such circumstances, many people who suffer from serious mental illness tend to withdraw. Former patients spend inordinate amounts of time at home with their families, live alone in a room, or are trapped in a jail cell. In effect, social isolation has become an all too common experience for people suffering from mental illness. While this group now lives in society and no longer in asylums, they are for the most part not really a vital part of that society.

Nor are we alone in this assessment. The editors of the *Psychiatric Services Journal* devoted the May 2012 issue to a review of social inclusion for people living with mental illness. They concluded that, while gains exist, the high hopes for advancing this issue have been disappointed. It is unimaginable that a society would deny patients upon leaving the hospital the rehabilitation services they need to support their productive reentry into society. And yet that is what occurs every day for people suffering from mental illness. While ample funding exists, principally through Medicaid, to address crisis episodes with hospitalization, most receive no form of ongoing rehabilitation. And people living with mental illness, who remain for the most part divorced from primary health care services, die on average 25 years earlier than the general public does (Parks et al., 2006). Suicide annually claims the lives of a significant number of people with serious mental illness. According to an October 9, 2006, World Health Organization news release, 90 percent of all suicides are associated with mental disorders. Michael Hogan, the chair of the President's New Freedom Commission on Mental Health (2002), summed up America's mental health service delivery system as "in shambles." In his interim report, he described the system as so fragmented that it allows too many people to fall through the cracks:

> We have found that the system needs dramatic reform because it is incapable of efficiently delivering and financing effective treatments—such as medications, psychotherapies, and other services—that have taken decades to develop. Responsibility for these services is scattered among agencies, programs, and levels of government. There are so many programs operating under such different rules

that it is often impossible for families and consumers to find the care that they urgently need. The efforts of countless skilled and caring professionals are frustrated by the system's fragmentation. As a result, too many Americans suffer needless disability, and millions of dollars are spent unproductively in a dysfunctional service system that cannot deliver the treatments that work so well. (p. 1)

It is disappointing to note that this concern repeats a similar public criticism that was raised decades ago when the U.S. General Accounting Office reported (1977) that patients with severe mental illnesses were being discharged into the community without adequate services to support their reentry into society. We suggest here that Fountain House, as a place for *community* in mental health practice, supplies a missing piece in the mental health policy puzzle that has been thwarting the functional recovery of people with a serious mental illness in society.

Loss of Place for Recovery

The idea of having a *place* for recovery—a niche, so to speak, in society—is not new in mental health practice. It was the original idea behind the asylums of the nineteenth century. Patients were removed from congested urban places, which were thought to precipitate their illnesses, and given refuge in the tranquillity of the countryside. These asylums gradually evolved, however, into the state mental hospital system, which by the late 1940s, while providing comprehensive medical and social care to people suffering from severe mental illness, had become overcrowded, underfunded, and hardly reflective of the humane and therapeutic approach of the moral treatment[2] upon which the institutions were originally patterned. With the introduction of psychotropic medications, the passage of the Community Mental Health Centers Act (Pub. L. 88–164) on October 31, 1963, and the subsequent waves of deinstitutionalization,[3] a new chapter was opened in the care and treatment of people suffering from mental illness. In the United States more than half a million people with severe mental illness moved from life totally spent in institutions back into their communities (Grob, 1994). Mental illnesses were no longer considered chronic, deteriorating diseases, and recovery from mental illness was now seen as a real possibility.

While it was right to do away with these bureaucratic nightmares, it was equally wrong not to replace them with adequate resources to help people with mental illness to live in the community. Deinstitutionalization was implemented without sufficient social supports in place and even less understanding of the impact that co-occurring conditions such as homelessness, unemployment, and drug addiction would have in their lives. Statistics reported by Klein (2006, p. 35) are alarming:

- Approximately 35% of homeless people are suffering from mental illness.
- The closing of inpatient psychiatric beds has resulted in the transfer of care from the hospital to other institutions that have not been able to adequately deliver effective services.
- U.S. jails and prisons currently house people suffering from serious psychiatric disorders in greater numbers than do public institutions.
- Discharge planning has not been successful in decreasing re-hospitalization over the long term.

And employment, which is the ultimate measure of success in recovery, remains elusive. Adults with serious mental illness face many challenges in attaining and retaining employment. As summarized by the President's New Freedom Commission's Subcommittee on Employment and Income Supports (2003), people with serious mental illness have the highest level of unemployment of any group with disabilities—fewer than one in five are employed. Unemployment occurs despite surveys showing that the majority of people with serious mental illness want to work and many could be working with assistance. This loss of productivity and human potential is costly to society and tragically unnecessary.

Nor does public funding for mental health services support the goal of recovery in society. Fifty years ago most mental health dollars supported the state mental hospital system. The majority of these hospitals have since been closed. In their place have emerged psychiatric wings in general hospitals, which concentrate on acute care and offer only limited access to community support services upon discharge. The largest share of current mental health dollars in New York State, for example, pays for inpatient beds located in general hospital units reserved for psychiatric and medical services for people with serious mental illness. Only a small portion of the dollars saved from closing the state mental hospitals has been retained to sustain community-based mental health recovery options.

At the same time, the states, as a cost-saving device, have shifted their mental health expenditures to federal reimbursements under Medicaid funding. Clearly, the reason for this shift is that the state then pays only a portion of the cost. (In New York, for example, the state pays 50 percent and the federal government pays 50 percent of costs.) The irony of this transfer is that while costs of Medicaid behavioral health care are still spiraling out of control, federal regulations attached to the funds severely limit the social service options and community support programs that could be made available to help people with serious mental illnesses survive in society. While we consider community support programs involving employment, housing, and education as key to a person's recovery, federal Medicaid laws, even under the rehabilitation option,[4] limit refundable activities regarded as educational or job-related. In sum, current public funding for mental health has created a dysfunctional system in which Medicaid-funded psychiatric services are costing more and more while the community support services, which are necessary to reduce these costs, are being depleted. Whereas government rhetoric says recovery in the community, federal funding is primarily promoting medical services in the hospital, ironically reinstituting the medical model as the primary intervention in psychiatric community support programming.

Nor will the new wave of managed care end such disconnects in the funding system. Government-managed care is designed to control Medicaid and Medicare expenses, paying solely for medical services. As long as most of the funding for mental health services is distributed through Medicaid or Medicare, the emphasis will remain on a medical model, and community support and recovery services will continue to disappear. This is occurring despite the promotion of parallel policies that combine psychiatric, medical, and community support recovery services to address the high health costs incurred by people with severe mental illnesses.[5] Last, as the states and the federal government reduce Medicaid coverage in order to save money, there is no state or federal replacement funding for recovery or community support services emerging on the horizon.

The real tragedy throughout this period, in our opinion, is the abandonment by state governments of their role to provide community support services to help those who are the most seriously ill. States are not reallocating the monies saved from closing state mental institutions and the subsequent transfer of mental health costs to the federal government. In effect, the states have abrogated their responsibility for mental health care and, under pressure to cut costs in public services, continue to reduce the funding that is necessary for the community support and recovery of people suffering with serious mental illnesses.

Thus, even though the idea that people with mental illness are able to live in the community was accepted decades ago, society has failed to provide anywhere near the range and depth of services needed so that those discharged from mental institutions can live in a meaningful and productive manner. Something is clearly wrong with the structure of the current system in addressing the needs of people with serious mental illness.

Purpose of the Book

This book does not provide a critique documenting the circumstances of this failure, nor does it investigate how it came about. Neither is it a history of the Fountain House community of West 47th Street in New York City, a place where the business of recovery has been a daily reality since its founding in 1948. Rather, this book is about Fountain House as a model for others to emulate. Decades ago a study team commissioned by the American Psychiatric Association and the National

Association for Mental Health came to assess Fountain House for this very reason. They were looking to study programs throughout the United States that seemed adept at meeting the employment, housing, and social needs of people living with serious mental illness (Glascote et al., 1971), and they selected Fountain House in New York City as among the foremost places to visit. While the study's authors were convinced that the large numbers of former mental health patients who had been discharged back into society under the rubric of deinstitutionalization had a right to live in society, they were equally aware of the realities of homelessness, unemployment, isolation, and hospital recidivism that the changeover had occasioned. The study team was intent on finding "a humane and socially useful approach to serving the mentally ill and enabling them to lead more productive lives in the community than had been possible before" (p. 5). They set out to ascertain what insight such programs could offer in defining a scalable support structure that would benefit previously hospitalized mental health patients in returning to a meaningful and autonomous life in society. The study commission selected Fountain House to investigate because it had acquired a noted reputation in this regard.

While the visiting team was impressed by what they found at Fountain House, they deemed its underlying conceptual framework—what staff described to them as a _family_—to be inadequate as a paradigm for broad-scale replication throughout the United States. To the researchers, the concept of family was "less a theoretical construction of rehabilitation than a vehicle for expressing a caring attitude towards clients" (pp. 17–18). They concluded that the successes achieved at Fountain House were more related to the enthusiasm and compassion of its staff than to any underlying replicable techniques and structures of a rehabilitative model. Fortunately others, largely field practitioners, were not so dismissive of what they observed at Fountain House, and realized the inherent power of its philosophy and practices for supporting the recovery of people living with mental illness. Fountain House went on to be replicated in hundreds of places, commonly referred to as clubhouses, throughout the world.[6] Nonetheless, the conclusion of the visiting observers in 1971 regarding the absence of a fundamental theoretical formulation is a weakness that we recognized in determining to write this book.

Previous Studies of Fountain House

Others have written about Fountain House. Most notably, Stephen Anderson (1998) chronicled the major events of the Fountain House story in his book *We Are Not Alone.* Flannery and Glickman (1996) published a series of member portraits and historical vignettes describing its operations, but not its theoretical underpinnings. In 1989, in response to a growing demand for replication of its program, Fountain House, in collaboration with other established clubhouses throughout the world, published a list of declarative statements, the standards for clubhouse programs, of what constitutes an authentic replication of the Fountain House model (Propst, 1992). The standards, however, were not designed to include any explanation of *why* people suffering from mental illnesses should be treated as prescribed by the standards, nor did they formally incorporate any scientific evidence supporting their effectiveness. While each of these texts, and others,[7] corroborate much of the material discussed in *Fountain House*, none provides (nor as far as we are aware does any other text) a unified conceptual framework that answers the question *why? Why do we do what we do?* The answer to this question is important, as it establishes not only the basis for the professional practice espoused by Fountain House for its staff and others in supporting the recovery of its membership, but also the grounds for affiliated frameworks in academia, research, and determination of public policy in mental health practice.

Fountain House, the book, is the story of a unique idea in mental health practice in which professionals and former patients gather every day and create a place that restores meaning in lives of those who have been marginalized in society by their illnesses, a place where the members and staff work together to find the resources within themselves and elsewhere for members to land a job, attend school, secure a home, and foster friendships. It is an idea that has inspired many with hope for recovery within society. *Fountain House* spins the theoretical threads that stitch together these various historical descriptions and personal accounts and explains their evolution into the present-day working community that is Fountain House. And as a disciplined methodology, it can be studied, replicated in practice, and used to speak directly to an impaired mental health delivery system.

Community as a Methodology

Fountain House espouses the construction of a working community as its signature approach to aiding members in their recovery from mental illness. The concept *community* is a compelling social construct, as it combines the vision of an inspiring ideal and moral imperative of how people should live together and treat one another with an empirical understanding of conventional group work processes where all the participants—members, staff, board, director, and extended band of volunteers—collaborate to work toward the central goal of supporting the psychiatric recovery of its membership. Thus, Fountain House represents both a posture, or ethic, about how people suffering from severe and chronic mental illness should be treated (i.e., as a member of the human community) and a methodology and rationale as to how such a vision is achieved.

In adopting community as a methodology, we make assumptions about the nature of mental illness that form the basis of our approach to supporting member recovery. Fountain House avows the social nature of our humanity. Consequently, we acknowledge that the loss of mutuality and the breakdown in relationships, which are attendant results of mental illness, have affected no group more profoundly than people suffering from mental illness. Moreover, the mere diagnosis of these diseases portends serious repercussions for patients in terms of the social stigma it conveys. Beard, Goertzel, and Pearce (1958) referred to the resultant alienation from family, friends, and coworkers, and the eventual isolation as "relationship failure." This social symptomatology of mental illness is what Fountain House seeks to redress.

Within an understanding of the relational destructiveness of mental illness, Fountain House embodies more than just a place of welcome and refuge. It features a systemic approach to helping people with the illness regain their lives. As a community with a therapeutic mission, Fountain House adapts task-group methodologies (Toseland & Rivas, 2011) to treatment outcomes. It redefines organizational structures, first shifting the focus of all treatments from the pathologies of patients (who at Fountain House are referred to as "members") to the resilience that they exhibit to engage in everyday activities as the path to their own recovery. Practically, Fountain House establishes itself as an intentional working community in which the need for member participation and choice in all matters empowers its members to take responsibility for their own recuperative progress as well as for that of others. Fountain House next calls for an alternative definition of the professional staff role for those working in the field of mental health. In its model, those with power join on an equal footing, side by side, with those who are systemically denied such status in the treatment of these illnesses. Thus, Fountain House offers an appealing professional alternative to those that are typically offered in society—one based on social justice, collaborative rather than prescriptive relationships, and personal judgment and initiative.

It should also be noted that just as collaboration dominates the practice methodology within Fountain House, partnerships frame its relationships with external agencies and organizations. Fountain House does not consider itself alone to be a comprehensive solution in the treatment of mental illness. In an early act of innovation, Beard reached out to businesses as partners in supporting the recovery of its members through the transitional employment program.[9] In acknowledging that we address the social aspects of the illnesses in question, we also recognize that there exists a place for others in the treatment and medication of those suffering from such illnesses as schizophrenia, bipolar disorder, or major depression. Our need to partner with other clinical agencies in this treatment is a topic that we will further explore in the afterword.

An important discussion throughout the book is the notion of community and its use in current mental health policy debates. While the word *community* appears in common treatments, such as Assertive Community Treatment (ACT) (Stein & Santos, 1998), its inclusion refers only to the location of the services, not the nature of the treatments furnished. It admits here to none of the relational qualities demanded of a working community as described in *Fountain House*. In contrast, we contend that the disregard for the relational nature of community on the part of current policymakers in mental health treatment only continues to reinforce the isolation and disillusionment brought about by deinstitutionalization. In this regard, we advocate the use of a community enterprise as a treatment methodology—where patients and professionals collaborate so that members survive and recover in society. In short, as our subtitle suggests, there need to be working communities in place as components of any broad-scale mental health recovery system.

Throughout this book, we cite the formative insights and practices of Fountain House's prime architect, John Beard. Put simply, Beard was an example of the power of indignation to breed invention. He believed in the human dignity of people who suffered from mental illness. He dismissed the idea that any person would be considered hopeless, and he avoided the inhumane manner in which people with mental illness were routinely treated in the mental hospital in which he worked. Driven by the mantra inculcated by his mother, "Do what must be done," Beard was determined to translate his understanding of the potentialities of people living with mental illness into opportunities that gave them hope. While Beard and the other Fountain House designers were not unaware of the pathological aspects of people suffering from mental illness, they chose instead to focus on what they termed their healthy behaviors. They felt that, beyond any basic need for food or shelter, people with mental illness needed *to feel needed*. Consequently, they built Fountain House as a strengths-based, opportunity-driven, collaborative organizational structure in which being needed and accepted is promoted, in an environment that communicates respect, self-determination, and empowerment. At Fountain House, people with mental illness are welcomed and encouraged to contribute their talents to the group as a means of helping themselves and each other to regain their lives, once lost to a destructive illness.

We know now that the Fountain House that John Beard built represented ideas and practices far ahead of his time. His approach presaged the current promotion of strengths-based (Rapp & Goscha, 2006; Saleebey, 1996) and empowerment (Simon, 1994) methodologies. Beard's practices are corroborated by current research into psychological constructs of self-determination (Deci, 1996; Deci & Ryan, 1985), as well as by Bandura's (1997) concept of self-efficacy.

Research has also been a significant component of the Fountain House approach since its earliest days. In the sixties and seventies, Fountain House designed and implemented two state-of-the-art studies (Anderson, 1998). The first showed the positive impact of its approach on reducing rehospitalization of people with serious mental illness. The second showed the need for intensive outreach into the community to better engage members in a working community. Staff continuously collected all forms of data in numerous small studies, even employing audiovisual recordings to document activities. Most significantly, Fountain House took part in a 2008 national study conducted under SAMHSA, the Employment Intervention Demonstration Program (EIDP), which examined the effectiveness of various forms of supported employment programs for unemployed individuals with psychiatric disabilities (Cook et al., 2008). The Fountain House study compared the job placement outcomes of Genesis Club in Worcester, Massachusetts, with those of a local ACT team. All the supported employment studies showed that people with mental illness could work if they were given the right support. Many of the studies, including the Fountain House study, showed that various forms of supported employment had good placement rates—in the range of 50 to 60 percent—but unfortunately the retention rate for all of the studies was low, around two months. The Fountain House study, however, showed that clubhouse-based supported and transitional employment jobs had the longest duration rates of any in the studies. The EIDP study contributed significantly to Fountain House and its clubhouse model's being added to the SAMHSA registry of evidence-based approaches, since it was an experimental study with a control group. An extensive body of research—the most significant being the employment study—in conjunction with papers submitted by the University of Massachusetts Medical School and the International Center for Clubhouse Development allowed the model to qualify and be listed with the registry.

Thus, Fountain House is more than a historical artifact or a program that John Beard invented. As we make clear throughout this volume, Fountain House is not limited to its place in space and time. Fountain House, the idea, was founded on several traditions that illuminate its theoretical and practice development. It originated as a mutual aid program for people discharged from state mental health institutions. As an offspring of the settlement house movement and more recently in terms of person-in-environment and generalist approaches in social work practice, Fountain House exemplifies authentic traditions of social work theory and practice whose outcomes have been rigorously substantiated. Finally, our understanding of "activity group therapy" (see chapter 1) is directly and profoundly influenced by the resurgence of the *traitement moral* under the generic name of *milieu therapy* that thrived in the United States during the mid-twentieth century. Fountain House thus combines both the activist and the empowerment structures of the consumer and settlement house movements with the recovery intent of humanistic, therapeutic thought. It is a practice whose flexibility to evolve and adapt has been proven through more than six decades of use. It offers inherent ideas and a vision that have attracted re-creations of its approach all over the world. It is a practice first formulated by John Beard and grounded in broader historical roots of mental health theory and practice. As a reinvention of Hull House for the twenty-first century, Fountain House holds a promise and hope for the future for people suffering from mental illness that are lacking in today's community mental health recovery delivery system.

The Organization of the Book

Fountain House is organized as a diptych. Part I clarifies the principles underlying the Fountain House working community approach; part II explains how these values and principles are realized in a unique and innovative professional application in mental health services—namely, its professional schema of social practice.

Our story begins in chapter 1 with John Beard, who in his second year as a graduate student in social work on field assignment in a psychiatric ward of a local hospital first came to understand the elements of an innovative task-group practice, activity group therapy (AGT). In AGT Beard established a prototype for a strengths-based and empowerment intervention in recovery exemplified in the best of social work practice today. Chapter 2 describes Beard's adaptation of the practice precepts he derived from AGT to Fountain House, which until the time of his arrival had operated as an amalgam of a settlement house for people suffering from mental illness and a consumer-run social club typical of the time period. Beard reshaped the tenets of task-group application represented by AGT into a more organic, recovery-oriented workday and after-hours social and recreational program. In chapter 3, we give definition to the functional nature of Fountain House as a working community in support of the recovery and social inclusion of people living with mental illness and discuss the central principles involved in its organization—namely, the *need to be needed*, the right of member *choice*, and the *collaborative* orientation of staff. These principles clearly draw into relief the difference between Fountain House as a communal effort and most other mental health agencies and services that organize themselves along an individualized service approach.

Part II of the book introduces in chapter 4 the methodology by which the Fountain House working community approach concretely manifests its values and principles—the application of *social practice*. Social practice seeks to restore the social networks of its members as an aid in their recovery. In this respect, we view Fountain House as a practice that is inspired by a vision, driven by the successes of its outcomes and continually submitted for review and innovation. We understand that social practice has two functional aspects: transformational design and motivational coaching. Chapter 5 defines transformational design and outlines how task-group methodologies as applied to the social milieu of a working community of the staff workers, members, and others in effect transform its structural ecology into numerous opportunities for participation and contribution in meaningful work on the part of the membership. Shared leadership in decision making (i.e., consensus decision making), modeling, and inspiring purpose are all standard tools in the hands of task-group facilitators at Fountain House. Fountain House further expects its staff to be effective agents of change in the community by advocating for social justice for its members. Chapter 6, on motivational coaching, defines the practice of one-on-one associations among members and staff. In their coaching role, staff are encouraged to initiate significant relationships with members to enhance the impact of feedback, remove impediments to participation, and increase risk taking in an effort to introduce members to groups and a community. Chapter 7 addresses practice issues such as maintaining professional boundaries or avoiding a debilitating dependency, which typically arise in the course of fostering significant staff–member relationships. It also explains the limits that confront a relational approach that is based on member choice. Finally, the afterword situates the Fountain House working community model within the current spectrum of mental health practices, with specific reference to dominant professional and consumer models. On a continuum of services, Fountain House represents a collaborative recovery center, a "place" in society that supports member recovery. We conclude with the description of an alternative comprehensive community mental health delivery system—a working community in partnership with a community health clinic (integrating physical and behavioral health and wellness) that is our vision for a comprehensive mental health delivery system for the future. Such undertakings will also create viable and rewarding roles for the medical and psychiatric professionals who serve in community mental health.

Who Should Read This Book?

We hope that *Fountain House* will appeal to a broad range of readers, even beyond those with a specific interest in Fountain House or the clubhouse movement that it has spawned. We expect readers to gain a conceptual understanding of Fountain House as a robust, humane, and conceptually fertile social endeavor in the service of people who live with mental illness. We intend this publication to open a dialogue with those institutions within society that study, practice, and initiate policy and treatments in mental health services. We acknowledge that our understanding of a working community and social practice, while grounded in experience, is rudimentary, and in continual need of reflection and adaptation. In putting our practice in language that is common to contemporary theories of mental health professionals, however, we hope to encourage a broader appreciation for ideas forged in previous centuries that can be brought to bear, as Fountain House has done, on improving the lives of those living with mental illness. We encourage others to join with us in a community methodology with the goal of bettering the lives of those suffering from this pernicious disease.

PART I

Working Community

John Henderson Beard

INSIGHTS FROM
ACTIVITY GROUP THERAPY

Moderate work and regular exercise restored him, in short time,
to the full enjoyment of his intellectual faculties.

—PHILIPPE PINEL, *A TREATISE ON INSANITY*

From 1950 to 1951, John Beard worked in Ward N-206 of the Wayne
County General Hospital. The hospital was known locally as Eloise,
as it was located in the Detroit suburb of the same name. The ward to
which Beard was assigned was populated by about 250 male patients
suffering from severe and chronic schizophrenia; no one thought any
of them would ever recover. At the time Beard was a second-year
graduate student in social work, doing his field placement assignment
at the hospital. It was during his time at Eloise that he was introduced
to a practice in psychiatric recovery that was to consume his imagination and energies for the remainder of his life.

At Eloise, Beard was wholly taken by the ideas of his supervisor, the
young psychiatrist Arthur J. Pearce. Pearce, like other mental health
reformers of the time, was appalled by the conditions in which people with mental illness housed in asylums were forced to live. Beard
and another colleague, the psychologist Victor Goertzel, learned from
Pearce that there was hope for recovery for people suffering from severe mental illness. They had adopted what we would consider today
a form of group work practice (Toseland & Rivas, 2011), which they
called *activity group therapy* (AGT). Pearce and his team believed that
AGT would restore the social functioning of their patients, a result

that in turn offered them the possibility of assimilation back into society upon discharge.

In 1958, the team published an account of their intervention in
an article titled "The Effectiveness of Activity Group Therapy with
Chronically Regressed Adult Schizophrenics" (Beard, Goertzel, &
Pearce, 1958). The article laid out the assumptions that guided their
intervention and the strategies that they found effective. Clearly, the
authors were energized by the successes that their approach had
achieved with the patients on Ward N-206. They asserted that a
reality-based, task-group methodology proved to be an effective treatment for even the most withdrawn patients suffering from mental
illness. For Beard, however, working at Eloise was a seismic event.
The insights he acquired from AGT went far beyond the immediate
successes in social reintegration with a small group of patients resid-
ing in Eloise. He was to apply a series of tenets he gleaned from AGT
for the remainder of his career. Thus AGT was the seed from which
Fountain House was later to emerge on West 47th Street in New York
City, and that in turn germinated into hundreds of clubhouses all over
the world.

AGT Treatment Design

The AGT team was not concerned with issues that normally consumed medical staff, such as differentiating the various illnesses
(namely, depression, schizophrenia, psychosis, delusions), identifying
their symptoms, or speculating on their etiology. They believed that
much of the suffering experienced by patients with mental illnesses
was the result of their isolation in society. Schizophrenia, in the team's
understanding, thwarted recovery by condemning patients to a life of
loneliness. The case histories of their patients, like the case histories
of most people suffering from severe mental illness, clearly illustrated
the devastating impact of psychotic behavior upon social relationships. Complications resulting from the patients' illnesses spilled over
into the social fabric of their lives, in many cases ripping it apart.

Estranged from family, unable to make friends, and besieged by the loss of jobs, failure in school, and ultimately homelessness, those suffering from mental illness succumbed to withdrawal, isolation, and, at times, conflict. Overt psychotic symptomatology, therefore, was not the only problem that such patients faced. If recovery was to take place, the team members reasoned, attention had to be paid to the destructive impact the illness had on the relational ties of the individuals and the social isolation that resulted. The team therefore expanded their notion of mental illness to include the breakdown in social relationships and defined the problem they would focus upon in treating individuals with severe mental illness in terms of isolation and the loss of the functional capacities of the individual to manage interpersonal relationships in ordinary living situations. They referred to the problem as "relationship failure" (p. 124).

At the same time, they were well aware that during World War II many psychiatric hospitals had depended upon patient labor as a way of remaining in operation. Patients went out into the fields to plant and harvest vegetables for meals, worked in the laundry rooms, and assisted in the kitchens. Likewise, although their patients on Ward N-206 were thought by many to be terminal, and therefore were relegated to remaining imprisoned in empty ward life, some of them demonstrated the ability to leave the wards and engage in ordinary productive activities. In other words, their patients were not wholly consumed by their illnesses. Patients appeared to retain intelligent areas that were fundamentally healthy and resilient. So, despite their illnesses, some of the patients were still capable of successfully engaging in collective endeavors. The observation provoked the assumption that there must be an aspect of the personality that, while latent, remained intact and unaffected by the illness and became activated when the patients left the hospital ward environment. The team referred to this capacity to join in ordinary human activities as "remaining ego strengths" (p. 125).

It was common at that time to describe the human personality in categories derived from Freud—namely, the ego, the id, the superego. In general, the ego was the conscious aspect of the person, which interacted with others and the environment. Intellectual functioning, such as cognition, reasoning, memory, and judgment, was considered to reside within the ego function. Focusing on the ego was pertinent in cases involving people who suffered from schizophrenia, since schizophrenia was essentially considered disruptive of ego functioning. As noted by physicians at the time (Freeman, Cameron, & McGhie, 1958), schizophrenia "is a disturbance of the development and maintenance of adequate ego boundaries which, on the basis of clinical observation, we have come to regard as the central feature of the schizophrenic disease process" (p. 49). With the inability to differentiate between internal thoughts and external realities, the loss of coherent thought patterns, or the erosion of social and other types of cognitive functioning, schizophrenia was considered to be, in effect, the loss of ego functioning of the individual.

On the other hand, when some patients left their hospital wards, they appeared to engage quite readily in activities with others. This observation convinced the team that there was an aspect of the person (i.e., ego functioning) that remained unimpaired by the illness. It prompted the speculation that if they could create an environment on the hospital ward itself that replicated these outside episodes—where the ego capabilities of their patients were not clouded by their mental illnesses—they could stimulate these healthy capacities, to the psychological benefit of their patients. They determined therefore to test the hypothesis—that participation in normal activities improved the condition of the patients—and introduced AGT on the ward.

Another factor also influenced the team's decision to implement AGT on the ward. They wanted to demonstrate that AGT was a generic approach that could be applied with even the most withdrawn patients, those who rarely, if ever, left the ward. Many programs sponsored in state mental hospitals of the time favored access to opportunities for work and recreation (Cumming and Cumming, 1962). Work, as Sacks (2009) has recently noted, could "normalize and create community, could take patients out of their solipsistic inner worlds" (p. 51). Opportunities for work, however, commonly took patients outside the hospital ward environs and were available only to those who were considered the most socially amenable—leaving the vast majority of patients to remain in gloomy back wards with no such privileges of access to varied and stimulating environments. Pearce and his team, therefore, chose to differentiate their intervention from those of their contemporaries by applying the practice of AGT on the ward. They sought to encourage their patients who remained on the ward to become involved in everyday group activities. If they were successful in engaging these most severely disabled patients in activity groups, they surmised, they could extrapolate their findings and apply them to larger populations of patients suffering from mental illness. Thus AGT was designed as a prototype of action research (box 1.1) (Argyris, Putnam, & Smith, 1985; Lewin, 1946; Stringer, 1999) in task-oriented group therapy. Despite patients' loss of relationships, the team observed, they retained capacities for normal work when they left the hospital ward. If the team could activate the healthy part of their patients (their ego capacities noted above) and engage individuals in ordinary group processes on the ward, they reasoned, they could rekindle the healthy capacities of the person, which though seemingly overshadowed by ward life still existed. As a result, patients would feel better about themselves. And, hopefully, some would find a way to get on with their lives outside the confines of the hospital. In this way the team introduced activity group therapy as their treatment approach and found that it had a salutary effect on the lives of their patients.

BOX 1.1.
The methodological design of AGT

Observation: People with mental illness exhibit "ego capacities" outside the hospital environment.
Hypothesis: Participation in task-group activities restores relational bonds.
Treatment: Various task-group activities (AGT) are introduced on hospital ward to draw upon patients' strengths.
Findings: AGT promotes recovery of people suffering from mental illness.

AGT also appealed to Pearce and his team because it provided a methodological framework to enlist all the people in the environment—including the hospital attendant staff and even fellow patients—in contributing to the recovery of people with mental illness. AGT created naturally interactive roles among the patients and the ward personnel. Linking the staff and other patients on the ward together in normal human activities (i.e., task-oriented group work), the team believed, would yield meaningful, empowering, and ultimately transformative results. Such a therapeutic application of task-group methodology was directly and profoundly influenced by the emergence of a popular humanistic form of psychiatric practice at the time, *milieu therapy*.

Resurgence of a Humane Psychiatric Treatment

Milieu therapy began as a reaction to the overcrowding and impoverished conditions that had arisen in the system of state mental institutions where by the mid-twentieth century most people who had been diagnosed as insane or mad were confined. It was accompanied by a resurgence of interest in the precepts of the *traitement moral*, or moral treatment, of the late eighteenth century. A number of pilot demonstrations (Greenblatt, York, & Brown, 1955) under the generic name of "milieu therapy" were undertaken in hospitals throughout the United States with the clear intention of restoring the enlightened and responsible psychological treatment of patients first promoted by the noted French physician Philippe Pinel (1745–1826).

Pinel's interest in caring for people who suffered from mental illness developed after the suicide of a close friend. Pinel attributed his friend's death to the gross mismanagement of the treatment he received. During the eighteenth century most remedies for mentally ill people who were not wealthy involved confinement and harsh treatment. As a citizen of the French Revolution, with its fresh understandings of the rights of mankind and freedom, Pinel believed in the humanity of all people, including those who were considered to be mad. Consequently, he viewed the harsh treatments that were meted out

8

to people with mental illness as unwarranted. He learned from Jean-Baptiste Pussin, the superintendent of Bicêtre Hospital (and former patient[1]), that patients were not without the capacity to respond with ordinary motives of hope and reason. Consequently, in his capacity as chief physician at various hospitals in Paris, Pinel advanced a systematic method of care for people afflicted with serious mental illness that favored a sensible approach (i.e., moral) over one of restraints (Pinel, 1806). Specifically, his approach involved close observation of his patients and therapeutic conversations regarding the illusions they verbalized. He also looked for their natural capacities and resilience that could support their improvement.

Pinel's significance extended beyond his therapeutic methodology, however. He complained, for example, about a hospital environment where

> the halls and the passages of the hospital were much confined, and so arranged as to render the cold of winter and the heat of summer equally intolerable and injurious. The chambers were exceedingly small and inconvenient. Baths we had none, though I made repeated applications for them; nor had we extensive liberties for walking, gardening or other exercises. So destitute of accommodations, we found it impossible to class our patients according to the varieties and degrees of their respective maladies. (p. 21)

Pinel wanted all aspects of the patient's environment organized with a therapeutic intent. He had the chains removed from his patients, and he replaced the dungeons in which they were forced to reside with an asylum where they were free to move around and enjoy the grounds. He advocated an enriched physical environment resembling a more normalized life that included purposeful activities, moderate work, regular exercise, and the selection of attendant staff whose benevolent encouragement would facilitate a therapeutic treatment.

In England Pinel's teachings regarding the humane treatment of patients suffering from insanity were mirrored by William Tuke, who founded the York Retreat, which applied Quaker teachings to the therapeutic treatment of mental illness (Tuke & Society of Friends,

1813). Like Pinel, Tuke was appalled by the mistreatment of a member of his Quaker community who suffered from mental illness. He was convinced that the conditions of her confinement contributed to her death. He was also influenced by the contemporaneous liberal ideas of John Locke and other political theorists who advocated for universal human dignity and equality. As a result, he determined that the treatment for people suffering from insanity must be offered within a framework that was consistent with our common humanity.

The humane and reasoned approaches of Pinel and Tuke soon found their way to the United States as part of the nineteenth-century innovation in the mental health service system, the asylum.[2] In the asylum, mental illness was considered treatable. The reformers advocated withdrawing the afflicted individuals from the commotions of ordinary life and locating them where they would be safe from the environment that they believed had caused the illnesses. They enforced a regimen to assist patients in the development of internal means of control so that their behaviors and values mimicked those of people in a normal society. Work was considered the "most efficacious" mode of treatment in this regard (Eddy, 1815, p. 9), as well as close, sociable relationships between the patients and their attending staff. Early adherents of the method required asylums to hire intelligent and sensitive attendants to work with patients, reading to them and talking to them, taking them for walks, and engaging them in other purposeful activities that were designed to distract them from what were considered irrational preoccupations.

A century later, however, most places providing treatment for the insane in the United States had fallen far from the humanistic ideals and medical quality of patient care represented by the enlightened thought of the moral treatment. By the mid-twentieth century, the state mental institutional system, where most people suffering from mental illness were now housed, had abandoned its societal function to restore patients to health and wellness. State mental hospitals had become warehouses of appalling conditions for over half a million people (Grob, 1994), most of whom were considered chronically ill. Their concomitant spiritual, emotional, and intellectual impoverishment only contributed to their deterioration and suffering. State mental institutions, in contrast to their general hospital counterparts, had become overcrowded, understaffed, and repressive institutions that regularly substituted the use of physical restraints for curative methods. Most patient care was virtually left in the hands of untrained custodial staff (Greenblatt, York, & Brown, 1955). So deplorable had conditions become that inadequacies in the number and preparation of staff in these hospitals, whose function it was to minister to sick minds, in contrast to general hospitals ministering to sick bodies, were so marked that "almost no general hospital would consider operation possible under the circumstances" (p. 1). In effect, society had all but determined that severe mental illness was chronic and those who suffered from it had no hope of recovery; consequently, they were not worth the bother.

In response, some in professional psychiatry looked back to the successes of earlier, moral treatment era for a solution. Adherents argued that recovery was possible and sought to change the notion of care for people with mental illness from subsistence maintenance to rehabilitation. They paid particular attention to reviving a relationally supportive social environment in the hospital for a therapeutic purpose—improving the capacity of patients for socialization. The treatment was termed *milieu therapy* (Rioch & Stanton, 1953). Proponents believed that milieu therapy, as a supportive social environment within the hospital, would have as beneficial an impact upon the patient's recovery as the dyadic relationship in traditional psychotherapy (Toseland & Siporin, 1986).

To achieve these goals, reformers expanded the treatment of mental illness by a few lone psychiatrists to include anyone who came in contact with patients (the nurses, the attendant staff, and even fellow patients), who constituted their social environment or social milieu, and thus could play a significant role in their recovery. A study of the phenomenon by the Russell Sage Foundation reflected the excitement at the time for the potential for patient improvement that *social treatments* promised: "Recognition of the inherent influence upon patients of every person who comes in contact with them, including the influence of patients upon one another, opens the door to an enormous broadening of the therapeutic potential over the most exclusive

reliance that has been placed upon somatic treatment and psychotherapy by psychiatrists" (Greenblatt, York, & Brown, 1956, p. 11).
Doctors believed that hospitals not only could become more inviting and humanitarian places, but also could be fashioned into a therapeutic platform in which the attendant staff and fellow patients could
be enlisted to provide support in the patient recovery effort. Milieu
therapy mirrored contemporary developments in England, known as
therapeutic communities and popularized by Maxwell Jones (1953)
in the Industrial Neurosis Unit of Belmont Hospital in London. Jones
avoided the restrictive and often demeaning practices of many psychiatric hospitals of his time. His central philosophy, like that of social
treatment practitioners in America, was to use "the whole hospital
community as an active force in treatment" (p. 157) and to have patients be active in their own and each other's mental health recovery.

The application of social treatments meant improving the physical
conditions of the hospital as well. The regimen typically called for
opportunities for work and recreation, which were always considered
to have a beneficent effect for psychiatric patients. As succinctly summarized by contemporaries of the times (Cumming and Cumming,
1962): work as therapy is both old and successful. In their opinion,
"chronic schizophrenics with long histories of deterioration have been
successfully rehabilitated and even returned to society through programs built around occupational retraining" (p. 231). While the im-
petus to include work as part of a mental health hospital regimen had
much to do with the need for patient labor to maintain these hospitals
during World War II, it still represented a staple of social treatment
efforts. Finally, with the shortage of trained psychiatric staff, special
attention also needed to be paid to the ward staff—the nurses, custodial attendants, outside specialists such as occupational therapists,
and even the other patients—as integral to achieving a therapeutic
impact in the intervention. And thus therapeutic teams with psychiatrists in their new role as team leaders of various staff rather than as
individual caregivers became a common mental health intervention.

It was at this point in time that the therapeutic team of Beard
and Goertzel, under the direction of the innovative young psychiatrist Pearce, came on the scene. They clearly saw themselves within

the broader context of the times, as part of a movement that was challenging a society whose indifference to people suffering from severe mental illness resulted in their confinement to the back wards of large, custodial institutions like Eloise. They recognized that the shift in emphasis they were advocating represented a clear break with the perception that these patients had little capacity, and even less hope, for recovery. In fact, they contended that the psychoses expressed by their patients had as much to do with an oppressive hospital environment, with its absence of substantive relationships, as it did with the afflictions of the illness itself (Stanton and Schwartz, 1954; Sullivan, 1931). They promoted in its place a humane, rehabilitative (rather than custodial) approach to the treatment of chronic mental patients.

As trained clinicians, Pearce and his team were familiar with the mechanics of forming and managing groups for therapeutic effect. Group therapy had long been acceptable, particularly in outpatient practice (Wender, 1936). But since AGT was organized as an intervention based on the health of patients, and not on their dysfunctions, its methodologies were not readily apparent or well understood. The authors in fact acknowledged that they were at a loss when asked to provide information regarding patient strengths. They admitted: "It was interesting to note how thoroughly we were able to describe many minute aspects of the patient's symptomatic behavior, but, when given the same task in reference to the patient's remaining areas of health, we were somewhat at a loss" (Beard, Goertzel, & Pearce, 1958, p. 124). AGT, therefore, involved inventing a hitherto uncharted approach for therapists to relate to their patients. Their task became to devise a structure for their relationships with their patients as individuals involved in constructive activities, rather than to cure a particular ailment or resolve a deficiency of some sort. The team therefore was intent upon identifying the constituent properties of the new relationships between the therapist and the patients, as well as among the patients themselves.

In the 1950s, and still today, there are mental health workers who follow a medical model approach; they diagnose their patients' deficits or needs and then devise a treatment plan. In contrast, Beard sought to identify an area of patient interest with which he could connect, structuring his intervention based on his patients' strengths. AGT was not just a moral or ethical statement that people with mental illness should be related to and treated as a person. It also represented a therapeutic technique with curative results that promoted the growth of lost or latent capabilities of those suffering from mental illness. Beard concluded that "when the activity structure is confined to occupations that bear relevance to the patient's strengths and capacities, the chances of 'relationship failure,' so often experienced in the past by patients, are greatly diminished" (p. 134). This emphasis on forming relationships by connecting with those areas of the patient's personality that were still healthy and normal represented an early example of what today is described as a strengths-based approach, which has become standard in today's mental health practice (Rapp & Goscha, 2006; Saleebey, 1996). Decades earlier, it had become a central element of the practice that Beard would subsequently introduce at Fountain House.

Learning a New Relational Approach

Due to the patient's tendency to withdraw and isolate, motivation was clearly the most immediate and challenging aspect of the therapist's new role in dealing with the person, and not the illness. The therapist needed to initiate the relationship-building process before facilitating participation in a group. As a first step, therefore, Pearce and his colleagues believed that by paying attention to the personal interests of their patients, they might be encouraged to join the activities on the ward. In every person there exists a natural resiliency or core of strengths, beliefs, and attitudes (referred to here as "remaining ego strengths," p. 125) which can be identified and made into the foundation of a general regimen for recovery. In developing relationships with patients, members of the team strove therefore to relate to these normal behavioral patterns and "utilize them actively in the establishment of a relationship between the patient and his environment in the hospital" (Beard, Goertzel, & Pearce, 1958, p. 124). The team found that even the most withdrawn of their patients demonstrated various behavioral patterns that, though seemingly insignificant, were still quite normal. Pearce therefore encouraged his colleagues to initiate their patient care by developing relationships with their patients—even the sickest among them, who stayed on the ward and could not go out on work release or for recreation—by connecting with their areas of personal interests and strengths.

Beard in fact went to extraordinary lengths in reaching out to his patients. For one patient, it was his interest in algebra; for another, his appreciation for food; and for a third, it was his preference for juvenile literature—each of which gave Beard a target to aim for in the relationship-building process. He surprised his patients, upsetting their routines, or behaving unconventionally in ways that conveyed a personal interest in them. He pursued one patient by getting to know him very slowly and arranging to meet with him on the hospital grounds over a six-week period. He wrote the names of his patients on the hospital ceiling, and asked each of them to point to his own name. He worked at odd hours, sometimes coming to the hospital at night and putting candy under a patient's pillow. He took walks with his patients, and showed acceptance of one, who had not spoken for years, by encouraging him when he said, "I have to pee," to do so publicly on the hospital lawn.

Needless to say, tension existed between the medical personnel on the ward and Beard and his colleagues. The introduction of even the simplest of changes was met by a lot of anxiety. Ward attendants at first thought that Beard was the one who was "crazy," and that chronic patients were not capable of properly handling what he was proposing. With painting, the attendants fully expected the patients to rip up the canvases. They could only use sandpaper and a piece of wood to introduce the woodworking shop. Gradually, however, the patients demonstrated their abilities to perform in a reasonable manner.

A challenge the team did face, however, as they reached out to the patients was whether they could keep their psychotic behaviors from actively intruding on forming a relationship with the therapist or from interfering when the individuals were integrated into groups. In other words, could the pathology of their patients be isolated without isolating the patients themselves? Beard explained: "In our effort to keep the patient's pathology socially isolated, but not the patient himself, we had to focus our attention on those remaining aspects of the patient's personality, which we believed to be the least pathologically directed" (Beard, Goertzel, & Pearce, 1958, p. 124). In this respect, Beard elucidated a powerful idea that symptoms do not constitute the person and that the patient is more than his or her pathology. If such a separation could be realized, it would leave the clinicians free to invite their patients to join in ordinary group activities.

As Beard sought to render pathology irrelevant in his relationships with his patients, he relied on the reality context of the relationships. For example, when William, one of his patients, would complain about being illegally committed to Eloise by his parents and declare how he would fix them when he got out, Beard would deflect such comments and differentiate his own interactions with William from those of William's parents. He emphasized that he did not know William at that time and that he would not, as his parents had, abandon him in the future. He would frequently express similar sentiments with his patients by disregarding their psychotic concerns and responding to them with statements evoking their personal intentions or dreams, saying that he would like to see them "ride their own horse" or "drive their own car." This is a central feature of a strengths approach—the aspirations of the individual hold primacy over the treatment as the centerpiece of the work (Saleebey, 1996). Thus, by staying away from pathology and by acknowledging and augmenting areas of personal interest, the team believed they could help their patients begin a process of re-establishing normal human associations. In this regard, activity group therapy proved especially robust, providing a reality context that at once avoided the illness and elicited client engagement.

Introduction to Groups

Once a one-on-one relationship had been established between the therapist and the patient, and it was clear that the psychotic symptoms were under control, the patient was introduced to a small group. Sometimes activities were as simple as playing catch with a ball. In another case, Beard, as noted above, persuaded an attendant who was a carpenter to bring some of his woodworking tools onto the ward and engage the patients in carpentry tasks. Stories were read in groups and the patients acted out the roles of various characters.

Activity groups were important to the process. Tasks that individuals performed as part of AGT in which patients could find success distracted withdrawn patients from their isolation, while offering other patients opportunities for coaching. The task groups were inherently empowering, providing a chance for taking on meaningful social roles from which participants in the group accrued self-worth and confidence. The team noted that acts of mutual aid began to emerge within the interactions of the group—the older members of the group began to help the more recent arrivals. Beard related a particularly memorable occurrence as the group acted out a scene from *Robinson Crusoe*, in which Crusoe was attempting to allay Friday's fears of being harmed. Harold, a normally quiet and somewhat inhibited member of the group, suddenly burst out with directions to John, who was playing the part of Robinson Crusoe: "Smile . . . of course . . . smile . . . and drop the gun." Beard commented upon the incident, "To our surprise at Harold's emotional direction to John, who seemed quite confused, John actually dropped the gun and attempted to put on a smile." Thus AGT was seen as establishing moments in which social networks became a resource for recovery beyond the relationship with the professional therapist. As the more capable within the group helped the more withdrawn, they earned for themselves status and feelings of self-worth.

Groups also provided an important role for the therapists, both as enablers in the situation and as models for normative social behaviors. In each group activity, Beard continued to relate to his patients personally and to involve them in interactions with one another. He felt that by getting into the act himself, he could direct the process much like an educator modifying the structure of the activities to promote the progressive learning of his students. As the group matured, visits to places away from the hospital became important to them. Beard

(1958) described a trip to a large cafeteria in downtown Detroit as follows:

> William exhibited a good capacity for selecting his dinner. Harold, however, became quite excited and could hardly pass up any item of food. Going through the line between William and the therapist, he first grabbed a shrimp cocktail, asking excitedly, "What is this?" He took soup and salad and practically every other item of food that he came upon. His tray was so full that he set his main dish on top of the cream pie. When he was seated at the table he seemed carried away and ate with his fingers, completely disregarding the utensils, stuffing his mouth full to the point where he could hardly chew. All in all he made quite a display. *The therapist made no comment about this and significantly, William, likewise accepted Harold's strange behavior* [italics added]. The curiosity of the other people in the restaurant did not seem to upset William, Martin, or John. Back at the hospital Harold made his first emotionally significant comment. "Thank you so much for taking me to the restaurant." Martin and John said they would like to go again. (p. 133)

Here the modeling behavior of the therapist had a profound effect upon the group. Instead of reflecting the unease of the other diners with respect to Harold's lack of manners (the public norm in the situation), Beard backed Harold's behavior in having a meal out on his own terms, for which he was grateful. He also set the example for the other patients on how to behave in the situation—a significant achievement to the team—so that the other patients indicated that they would enjoy returning as well.

AGT was essentially a collaborative approach that emphasized the association of both the professional and the patient with a common goal. The therapist had a specific role in the process: contributing to the ongoing development of the group, sustaining its momentum, modifying the group's activities as behaviors evolved into more mature social patterns. Beard viewed this collaboration as constructive, empowering, and ultimately transformative.[3]

Choice was another fundamental aspect of AGT. The fact that activities could be set up on the ward meant that the patients were
free to choose whether or not they wanted to participate in them.
Beard's patients did not have to go through the permission process of
the hospital for a day pass to work off the ward in the community.
Patients did not have to prove that they would behave themselves to
participate. There was no readiness test. For Beard and his colleagues,
if a patient wanted to participate, he or she needed only to ask. The
voluntary nature of participation was another condition of effective
treatment when attempting to connect with the healthy part of the
person. As the team observed: "We believe John was 'soaking us up'
in the first three sessions and his coming to the table on his own was
an indication of a real internally motivated 'reaching out.' This we
believe is the first step that has to be made before a patient can receive
any benefit from a group experience" (Beard, Goertzel, & Pearce,
1958, p. 130). The team believed that patient improvement depended
upon the patient's free and active engagement in the group's activities.
Patients had to start to take responsibility for their own actions. It
is the same power of personal choice that is so effective in recovery
efforts.

As time passed, the frequency and level of interaction and participation in each group progressed and the behavior of the group
members improved. Eventually, as group members took on more responsibilities, they spent more time away from the hospital. At this
point, Beard introduced his most imaginative programmatic achievement yet: taking advantage of employment opportunities with local
businesses to give patients the experience of working at real jobs.
Beard's role was to find employment nearby and to offer the support
that his patients needed to succeed, such as on-the-job training and
coverage when they were sick. Employment as a programmatic tool
was an important step in the process of preparing patients to return
to their home communities after hospitalization. In addition to setting
the stage for transitional employment, this step in the process introduced the function of ultimately connecting members in the group
with real employment as a path to social inclusion in the community.

Insights from AGT

The impact of Beard's mentorship under the guidance of Arthur Pearce cannot be overstated. He was wholly taken with the insights he gained at Eloise—that real recovery exists even for those who are deeply disturbed psychotically and that their participation in everyday group activities can have a curative impact. The methodology that resulted was thoroughly suffused with the guiding ideal of hope, which had been essentially lost in the expansion of the state mental health hospital system. The task-oriented group work of AGT provided a way of circumventing the patient's pathologies (in effect rendering pathology irrelevant) and tapping into or reactivating those residual "ego strengths" that appeared to exist in the patients. AGT also confirmed that individual human support and encouragement from a psychiatric social worker were essential in the recovery process. These produced a set of specific insights and techniques that would be useful for structuring such future interventions (box 1.2). In other words, the intervention not only detailed a set of values that is consistent with today's standards in mental health interventions—namely, an empowerment approach to patient recovery that accommodates patient initiative and choice. It also unearthed a kernel of a methodology that reflected a person-in-environment approach, which personifies exemplary social work practice (Kemp, Whittaker, & Tracey, 1997). The methodology employed a set of practical strategies informed by a personal understanding of the nature of the illness that patients were experiencing—the loss of relationships and its resulting isolation—as well as the resources within the community that could be employed to foster a recovery, the formation of normal activity groups.

Specifically, AGT sought to link patients with a social network that became supportive of their efforts to regain their natural capacity for engaging in society. The team developed strategies to overcome the challenges involved in motivating patients—anxious and isolated though they were—to participate in group activities. They were expected to initiate a process and reach out to a population whose illness was marked by relationship failure and social isolation.

BOX 1.2.
Practice tenets of AGT

- foster participation in ordinary human activities (task-group methodology)
- connect with patient interests (strengths-based)
- respect patient self-determination and choice (collaboration)
- open pathways to employment (social inclusion)

Rather than offering a prefabricated plan of action, the team determined that there had to be something that genuinely piqued patient interest, to which they would respond. In the search for this key, the team came to appreciate the way access to choices left room for client self-determination and empowerment. Practically speaking, they were developing specific strategies that have come to be associated with a strengths-based approach. And then, once individual patients merged into groups, the team assumed a more inventive role as creators of ever broader opportunities for patient empowerment and involvement and models of normative behaviors.

Finally, the system within which they worked was not closed. It functioned as an instrument of social inclusion and held out the promise of eventual return to society by including opportunities for employment in the community. Clearly with these tenets in mind, Beard and the others on the clinical team discovered for themselves what others have since recognized as essential elements in any intervention supportive of mental health recovery—namely, that exemplary recovery programs are strengths-based, empowering, collaborative, and employment-oriented.

Beard, Goertzel, and Pearce were all excited about their successes with their patients and concluded that participation in group activities resulted in varying degrees of patient improvement. They broadly summarized their success by noting that "the patient's new experience in participation with others on a basic reality level seems to promote a process of reinstituting lost ego capacities; and that 'AGT' can play an important part in facilitating adjustment in the community, thereby potentially lessening the probability of re-hospitalization" (1958, p. 136). For Beard personally, the insights acquired amid the desolate conditions of a custodial mental hospital ward in 1950 preoccupied him for the rest of his professional life. He was captivated by the righteousness they represented and driven by their clarity. As he reflected years later about his experience at Eloise and his subsequent leadership at Fountain House (Beard 1978), he understood that his career was all "part of a fabric . . . and once you get on that trip it becomes inevitable. You don't have choices any longer about what you're going to do about a whole host of things" (p. 4). For Beard, AGT provided both the moral imperative to activate the unforeseen human potential in a population who lived with a severely stigmatized illness and a set of tenets that would guide his actions in pursuit of his vision throughout his life.

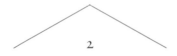

2

REINVENTING
FOUNTAIN HOUSE

You can't befriend a person into wellness . . . I also need to
engage in something from which I can derive my own sense of
pride, accomplishment and self-satisfaction from inside.

—SUSAN OMANSKI, MEMBER OF FOUNTAIN HOUSE

Fountain House was established in 1948 amid high hopes of providing a supportive community for patients who had been discharged
from mental hospitals. The board of directors was incorporated as
the Fountain House Foundation and promptly put together a funding
package to purchase an attractive building on West 47th Street in mid-
town Manhattan to house the new program. Those who participated
at Fountain House were called members—no longer patients. The
membership was organized under the Fellowship, which was separately incorporated, and operated as a social club typical of its time
(Carmichael, 1959). The Fellowship provided mutual support for its
members through discussions, dances, and other forms of social and
recreational events. In the following year, a small staff was hired.

Initially, Fountain House functioned much like a settlement house
for people suffering from mental illness.[1] Indeed, this image of itself
was underscored at the time by its name, Fountain "House." Its origin
was comparable to that of settlement houses. It was launched by a few
wealthy volunteers who joined with a group of ex-patients from a state
psychiatric hospital. The original mortgage on the building was held
by Hartley House, a settlement house abutting Fountain House from
an adjoining street. Even beyond these casual associations, however,

Fountain sculpted by Saint Clair Cemin in the backyard patio of Fountain House

the early Fountain House clearly functioned like a settlement house of the mid-twentieth century.

Fountain House as a Settlement House

It is not surprising that Henry Steele Commager characterized the emergence of settlement houses in the urban and industrial slums of the late nineteenth and early twentieth centuries—such as the Henry Street Settlement in New York City or, most famously, Hull House in Chicago—as "one of the great social movements in modern America" (Addams, 1961, p. xi). It was not only that they attempted to ameliorate the intertwined problems of immigration and poverty. Rather, it was the dashing manner in which they sought to accomplish these ends that so inspired the hundreds of replications of their endeavors. As a group, settlement house workers were driven by a sense of social justice in response to the exploitation of a vulnerable population, and they willingly shed their own trappings of status to "settle" and live with the people whom they wanted to help become productive citizens.

Settlement houses were not so much organized programmatic incursions as they were practical responses to the immediate troubles at hand: the social workers who practiced in settlement houses were proactive problem solvers. Immigrants were taught to read English; people learned about nutrition and cooking; nurseries were founded for working mothers; child health centers and work centers were opened, providing social services, training, and recreational activities. In these endeavors, settlement house workers broadly adopted what we would now term a "person-in-environment" approach (Bartlett, 2003), which recognized the interplay of societal expectations and norms as determinant of choices and possibilities for the individual. In that analysis, it was necessary to change societal structure in order for poor immigrant populations to see improvement in the quality of their lives. Thus, settlement house workers took prominent positions on such issues as fighting for labor laws on behalf of children and women or lobbying local governments to provide public bathhouses, neighborhood parks and playgrounds, branch libraries, and better waste collection.

In this respect, settlement houses functioned not only as agents of development, expanding access to the services normally provided to more wealthy citizens within society, but as vocal agents for structural change, seeking to reshape society at large. In contrast to the charitable associations of the time, which were the precursors of today's social workers, they were not content with simply resolving the pressing problems of the poor. They considered much of the blame for the situation to lie with obstructive legal policies and exploitive industrial practices of society at large, rather than with any moral failure of the immigrants. The settlement house movement, in effect, represented social justice, not charity, and emphasized the correction of social conditions that led to poverty over the moral redemption of the individual (Davis, 1984).

In helping people in need, the settlement house movement played a formative role in the development of social work practice. Central to its mission was the view that the poor possessed personal resources that, with help, they could use to improve their circumstances. The movement addressed head-on the problems of health, education, and employment caused by urban overcrowding and poverty and at the same time empowered the people to stand up for themselves. As Husock (1992) observed, their mission was like furnishing "a community living room" (p. 55), where everyone in the neighborhood could come with their personal needs. Instead of direct counseling, people were helped by encouraging them to assume an active role in the community. Thus, in addition to helping with the provision of educational, employment, and medical support, advocacy, and recreational activities, workers also sought to empower the poor to take control of their own lives. This nonpaternalistic attitude on the part of settlement house workers emphasized an empowerment ideology that is a major tenet of social work practice (Simon, 1994) and that remains a key value and programmatic feature of Fountain House today.

The early Fountain House, like the settlement house movement, incorporated an empowerment approach, with members banding together under a patient-directed Fellowship for their mutual benefit (Robbins, 1954). Members were thought to possess the personal resources that they would need to improve their circumstances and be a special help to one another because of their common experience. Fountain House also offered the normal fare of educational and social programs typical of settlement house operations. For example, with the support of Rockland State Hospital, it conducted an occupational therapy class (held in the adjacent Hartley House because of insufficient space at Fountain House). Fountain House was also awarded a contract by the New York State Department of Vocational Rehabilitation to train members in skills that would prepare them to assume clerical positions in businesses. Finally, the spirit of the original settlement house workers in valuing *settling* among the people they wished to help still exists in Fountain House today. Granted, Fountain House staff do not physically reside with the members—each returns at the end of the day to his or her own home. But, as generalists, Fountain House staff are expected to associate with members in a wide range of situations, from working together, to eating together, to learning a job together, to playing baseball games together, to traveling and rooming together. Fountain House does not limit the interactions of its professional staff and clients according to some definition of the treatment to be offered, nor does it prescribe a professional code of ethics that precludes these types of associations. Rather, effective social practice at Fountain House demands a range of associations, viewing all of them as essential to overall effectiveness of the staff role in a helping relationship.

In sum, Fountain House, as its name implies, represents a settlement house for those with mental illness and as such reflects an authentic and historical aspect of social work practice. Fountain House functions the same way today for people living with mental illness as settlement houses did for the poor in a previous century. Fountain House is a "settlement," or a place in the community, where professionals and their clients who suffer from mental illness associate widely with one another in seeking ways to empower members to move on with their lives.

The traditions of the settlement house movement, however, were not the ones upon which Fountain House was ultimately to be conceptually designed. With the arrival of John Beard in 1955, the basic foundations of Fountain House were wholly recast according to the tenets of AGT and milieu therapy, which traced its historical roots to the humanistic tradition for madness of the late eighteenth century, the moral treatment.

The Arrival of John Beard

John Beard first heard of Fountain House from a colleague in an outpatient clinic in downtown Detroit, where he was employed after earning his master's degree in social work. He was intrigued by the description of Fountain House as a clubhouse run by its membership, and he stopped by to see it for himself on a visit to New York in January 1955. He was excited that Fountain House offered the chance for him to demonstrate his activity group approach for post-hospitalized adults. But what he found at Fountain House when he assumed his position of director on June 1, 1955, was not what he had expected.

With the experience of Eloise fresh in his mind, John Beard arrived intent on implementing the techniques for group therapy that he had absorbed at Eloise. He was shocked to find, however, a community bitterly divided and at odds within itself, a community that frustrated any attempt on his part at connecting with the membership. Conflicts raged between the staff and the board, between members and staff, between members and the board, and among the members themselves. The previous director had resigned at the request of the board of directors. One of the other full-time professional staff workers left just before Beard's arrival, and the third professional left one month later. After the secretary also left, only two part-time social workers remained. While the board was successful in raising money privately, government funding had all but dried up. The events of this period are recounted in Stephen Anderson's book *We Are Not Alone* (1998).

The conflicts centered on the activities of the Fellowship, the member organization within Fountain House, which had been conceived as a mutual aid association, separately incorporated but under the legal auspices of the Fountain House Foundation. One issue, among others, was the role of staff workers. Leaders within the Fellowship advocated a separatist approach in which members shunned working with a professional staff—an approach that still exists today in some consumer-run and peer-support organizations (Borkman, 1999; Pulice and Miccio, 2006). Beard felt that such sentiments were needlessly divisive, especially given the successes of the collaborative approach among the professionals and their patients that he had seen achieved at Eloise. The Fellowship also employed an electoral process to determine which members would conduct the various activities of the clubhouse. In effect, the Fellowship, made up entirely of people with severe mental illness, had adopted a programmatic stance that resulted in winners, those who would manage the various operations, and losers, those who were denied such opportunities. Beard found such a situation odious for an organization that was intended to provide rehabilitative services to everyone. Eventually, in the summer of 1956, he disbanded the Fellowship. On the day following the dissolution, he reopened the front doors of Fountain House with a new approach, one marked by his own vision. Beard emphasized the development of mutually supportive relationships among members and staff in the context of carrying out meaningful everyday tasks in maintaining the house. Ironically, Beard was reviving the practice of mutual aid among members that had first inspired WANA, the *We Are Not Alone* Society, from which Fountain House emerged (Anderson, 1998) but had been lost in the Fellowship.

Designing Fountain House

From the moment he first set eyes on Fountain House, Beard was taken with its potential. Fountain House, he exclaimed, "sat vacant" and could be molded to his liking. With the Fellowship now disbanded and with a change of venue from a hospital to an urban setting, where the culture of illness no longer prevailed, Beard grasped the opportunity to create the type of constructive social interaction among members and staff, as well as among the members themselves, that he believed would foster patient recovery. The moment that crystallized this transition for him occurred when Mary Smith, a social worker at Fountain House, gave him a fresh way to think about using the empty space (Beard, 1978).

One day Mary Smith invited members to join her in preparing lunch in the downstairs kitchen at Fountain House. The task of making lunch and cleaning up afterward—activities that touched the immediate needs of members—constituted an essential ingredient of AGT. When group activities at Eloise were centered on everyday interests (such as carpentry, painting, or playing catch), they elicited enthusiastic responses from the patients. Beard concluded that the framework of a workday organized around preparing food, answering the phone, or helping with housing held broad potential for what he wanted to achieve in the therapeutic application of group activities.

Workday-like group activities offered meaningful and easily accessible roles that members could assume in the running of the house, with staff playing a vital part in the process.

Involvement in everyday work made sense to Beard. He thought that real work reflected a more meaningful experience of life than, say, attending a baseball game. He believed that work constituted much of life[2]—he himself was accustomed to working seven days a week. Work also had an inherent value that in Beard's mind would naturally attract people to participate and contribute their talents. At Eloise, for example, he met with his patients in an unused storeroom. Such an area provided a venue separate from the attitudes and concerns of the hospital staff where Beard could, as he explained, "engage in issues people could respond to." Here he would play catch with a ball or read passages from a McGuffey Reader (Beard, 1978, p. 9). His interactions in the storeroom were indicative of his approach of seeing his patients not at their worst but at their best, and appealing to something that they found interesting and at which they could succeed. Similarly, a schedule framed around a workday would achieve at Fountain House the same thing that the storeroom accomplished at the hospital: the establishment of a series of daily tasks and activities to which individuals could contribute and in which they could find meaning and purpose for themselves. As Susan Omanski, a member of Fountain House, later observed, she needed "to engage in something from which I can derive my own sense of pride, accomplishment, and self-satisfaction from inside" (Waters, 1992, p. 42). Thus the workday became the organizational scaffolding at Fountain House around which the members and staff could join forces daily in maintaining the house and carrying out its restorative function for the membership.

Work was also a normalizing factor for Beard. "Normalcy" represented a powerful word in Beard's vocabulary, one that resonated with his contemporaries in rehabilitation (Wolfensberger, 1972). There was nothing unusual about going to work. By expecting members to show up for work at least five times a week, Beard wanted to send the message that members would be treated the same as everyone else in society. The workday framework at Fountain House provided the reality basis that was so essential for Beard's intervention. While not denying their illnesses, Beard—as did the practitioners of task-group methodologies who trained him—had found in the workday the engagement in ordinary human pursuits that appeared to bypass the illness with its distractions and crippling negativity and that let members become involved with others. The day program, as it was referred to at the time, centered on work. By framing Fountain House as an ordinary workplace environment, with opportunities for recreation and socialization after hours, Beard was in essence reinventing for the membership of Fountain House the same potential for a natural restorative setting that had shaped his successful intervention in Eloise.

In addition to its programmatic import, the concept of normalcy also framed Beard's relationship with his patients. He was not going to assume the traditional role of the mental health worker who studied the contours of these illnesses and the etiology of their impact upon the individual. Instead he staked out a different, non-medicalized, role for himself. He was eager to pursue with members their "issues of personal freedom" in a normal environment. He focused on those aspects of their personality that were still healthy (or as he referred to them, their residual ego strengths) and that permitted them to participate in ordinary human activities.

Fountain House, conceived as a normal place of work, also held a demonstrative payoff regarding what Beard hoped to achieve. If the members of Fountain House were doing normal things, then they just were not as sick as society deemed them to be. And society would be forced to acknowledge this. Beard indeed did challenge the status quo in society, but not as an activist community organizer; his approach to change was demonstrative rather than confrontational. The reality of his patients' engaging in normal activities clearly made a statement about their inherent worth and sanity. Fountain House, by its very presence, he believed, would challenge the prejudices associated with mental illness and prompt a reevaluation of how people diagnosed with mental illness were to be viewed.

In effect, Fountain House had become a wholly secularized version of what Beard had tried to achieve in the therapeutic application of group activities in the hospital. Stripped of its medical trappings and its preoccupation with illness, the workday at Fountain House provided a natural setting for self-initiated social interaction and personal contributions in which the collaboration of staff and patients in everyday activities was transformative and held out the promise of aiding patient recovery.

Structuring the Day Program

Beard moved aggressively to restructure Fountain House around a normal workday. He viewed isolation in the community, with its accompanying sense of fright and insecurity, as the most dysfunctional factor that discharged patients had to face. A workday that invited members to join others in responding to one another's recovery needs, with the attendant implications for discovering personal meaning and satisfaction, became a tool to lure them out of their isolation. Fountain House opened its doors at nine in the morning and closed them at five in the evening, five days a week, just like a normal place of business. Beard divided the house into various task areas: doing clerical work, making lunch, cleaning and repairing areas. Members who participated gained the experience of being able to do things that had meaning for others. For example, Anderson (2005, p. 28) reported that members in the clerical area had provided remarkable assistance to the secretaries, coming in at nine in the morning and working until they left at five. Staff saw that these and other members were working at the level of normal employees, and began placing them in jobs at local business establishments, even though many of them had not successfully worked for a number of years. Finally, recreation-oriented groups, like drama, poetry, and art (typical daytime activities in partial and day hospital programs), were shifted to social and recreational activities scheduled in the evenings, on weekends, and on holidays.

The People Who Make Up Fountain House

The formation of Fountain House as a place of work also gave definition to the major roles of members, staff, and others who would function within its walls. While operating within a framework based on work, Beard rejected the highly specialized division of labor that typifies contemporary organizations, including mental health agencies. He chose instead to base the programmatic aspect of his organization on two simple, highly flexible functional categories of participants: members and staff workers. Members were free to choose how they would participate in terms of their own recovery goals, and staff were expected to reach out and engage the members in the daily operations. In these efforts, however, members and staff were expected to work together, side by side, in the daily operation of the house, in effect sharing responsibility for running the house.

As discussed earlier, in the AGT model, patient participation in activities at hand is crucial to the recovery process. The staff employed any and all activities within the community as opportunities for motivating member participation, and supported member involvement through the removal of impediments to their participation and the recognition of their achievements. As a new staff worker at Fountain House in 1964, Julius Lanoil began his work assignment in the day program by starting a thrift store in a place that had been rented for this purpose, located on Ninth Avenue around the corner from Fountain House. His assignment included maintaining a caseload of members, finding jobs for members, and overseeing apartment residences. He was also responsible for planning and running the Wednesday evening social program, and once a month he was scheduled to work on the weekend recreational program. Finally, he was expected to attend the daily four o'clock wrap-up with John Beard and bimonthly discussions with Mary Smith for clinical supervision. In his notes about his experiences at Fountain House, Lanoil described his first harrowing week on the job as a new staff worker:

> The store needed to be decorated, outfitted with display cases, and who would do the merchandise pickups with our van. How could the store be covered from 10 am to 4 pm, five days per week (the initial store hours), and who would do the pricing, the tagging, and the advertising? It was at this point that I began to understand what Fountain House was all about. And, as I reached out

to members, I was gratified with each "yes" that I received. Over time, the work assignments were broken down into various parts managed by myself and a group of about twenty members. Every morning our group met to plan the day's activities, check the status of an ongoing project, plan a reaching out to a homebound member, orient new members, discuss the happenings in the Fountain House community in general and give positive feedback and support to members of the group.

As is clear from this account, although the tasks at hand appeared overwhelming, it was the collaborative nature of the endeavor that made it all possible. Lanoil commented further: "Today when I hear staff talk about their need for more staff in a work group or unit, I say 'no you don't.' It's the enormity of the job and the fact that you can't do it alone that creates the therapeutic opportunities that make the Fountain House model unique and effective."

Other roles at Fountain House included those of the director, who held the ultimate responsibility for all community operations, and the board of directors, who held fiduciary responsibility and provided access to broader resources and support in the community to ensure the long-term identity and sustainability of Fountain House.[3] Finally, as a social agency deeply committed to the health and welfare of its members, and people suffering from the stigma of mental illness worldwide, Fountain House attracted numerous individuals who volunteered their time to work within its community structure or provided financial support as donors.

Anyone associated with Fountain House assumes one of these several identifiable roles: member, staff, director, board member, or volunteer. Even today, while Fountain House has grown into a large social service agency with approximately 1,200 members annually and 70 staff workers,[4] each participant, with some variation, belongs to one of these broad functional categories as designed by John Beard. Together, the members, staff, director, board of directors, volunteers, and donors who constitute the Fountain House community can be observed to be actively engaged in the fundamental structures of social life in an organization, the pursuit of various roles with a manifest

sense of purpose (Biddle, 1986). And every clubhouse that has replicated the Fountain House approach comprises the same set of actors,
all in pursuit of supporting member resiliency in the face of mental
illness.

Societal Integration: Employment and Housing

The Fountain House that Beard redesigned featured area work groups
in which participation was considered pre-vocational in intent and
suitable for patients recently discharged from a psychiatric hospital
(Goertzel, Beard, & Pilnick, 1960).[5] Beard did not oppose programs
that taught job-related skills, but for him there was no substitute for
a non-simulated, real job in a real place of business for equal wages.
He explained: "Wouldn't it be nice for evaluation to also include what
the reaction is and behavior in a real work situation, where all the
variables are normal? You can practice, I suppose, with a tennis racket
up to a point in places other than a tennis court. It would still seem to
me that you got to get on that court. It's got to be a real one to see,
you know, how you are doing" (1978, p. 22).

He found, however, that for many members, personal capacity development at Fountain House was not enough. With long hospitalizations, no recent job experience, and residual insecurities, many members lacked the wherewithal both to handle the competitive hiring
process and to successfully master on their own the tasks that were
expected of them in the workplace. Some members were afraid to
go out and find a regular job. Employment in regular jobs had always been Beard's eventual objective (he eschewed programs that had
no direct links to employment), and he considered it "deplorable"
for rehabilitation programs to be closed systems, like imprisonment
without any hope of returning to society. At the same time Beard
was realistic enough to understand the extent to which stigma in the
workplace affected people suffering from mental illness. "Businesses,"
he commented, "were not banging down his doors" to hire people
recently discharged from a mental institution. Something more was
needed. If eventual member employment was to be the outcome of

Fountain House, it would have to broaden its scope and take on the task of directly assisting members with finding employment. In transitional employment, jobs were provided for Fountain House members in regular places of business.

Beard, borrowing from his earlier practice at Eloise of securing employment for his patients from local businesses, reached out again and tapped the vast potential of local establishments in New York City to support the vocational aspirations of the membership. The resulting program, started in 1958, was initially called the Employment Placement Project. A brochure prepared by Fountain House introduced it thus, as quoted by Anderson (1998):

> Having made a good vocational adjustment within the Fountain House environment, the patient now looks to employment within the community. This is what he has been building up to. Only one more step is necessary. To assume regular full-time employment, a "transitional experience" is required. The employment placement project of Fountain House is designed to provide this type of experience. (p. 29)

The signature label for the initiative, *transitional employment* (TE), came one or two years later.

In transitional employment, Fountain House would extend its reach into the workplace in a manner that would benefit both the employer and the member. The jobs were not specially created for Fountain House; an employer was usually asked to give Fountain House one or more of the regular ongoing jobs. Since the purpose was to provide a training experience in the generic aspects of work, not job-specific training, TE jobs did not require any complicated technical expertise. Placements included messenger work at a small printing company, file work for a brokerage firm on Wall Street, clerical work in a large department store on Fifth Avenue, assembly work in a drug-packaging firm, and stockroom work in a wallpaper factory. A staff worker from Fountain House first learned the job and then accompanied the members to the job, introduced them to the relevant personnel on the job, and trained them in the tasks involved, remaining available through-out to assist them as needed. Fountain House thus had complete re-sponsibility for choosing the clients and promised the employer daily full and efficient coverage of the work. This promise of coverage made by Fountain House became a strong initial selling point to the em-ployer and provided the basis for the emerging partnership between Fountain House and the employer in a member's recovery.

Once the employer agreed to hire a member, Beard felt he had circumvented the major hurdle faced by people with a mental health history in a competitive hiring process. It eliminated the job interview. This was the key, as he asserted:

> I think basically . . . it completely bypasses, surgically removes, if you will, it makes irrelevant the history of mental illness. It is as if it didn't exist. It similarly just bypasses the absence of a successful work adjustment, the absence of any work adjustment, or the pres-ence of a terrible work adjustment. It just completely eliminates it. In other words, if those are barriers to having a chance to go to work, those barriers don't exist because by definition transitional employment completely removes them. You don't have to pass a job interview. (Beard, 1978, p. 19)

At the same time, transitional employment was designed to teach the basic skills involved in competitive employment to those who had lost or never learned the generic skills necessary to be successful in a competitive job.

Members typically worked on any one TE from three to four months,[6] which was considered a reasonable timeframe for a member to learn generic work skills before moving on to independent employ-ment. During this initial period, members were expected to maintain regular attendance and learn appropriateness of dress and hygiene, how to relate to an employer and other employees, how to deal with personal fears and symptom management, and how to communicate and initiate an action on the job. Having belief in oneself and master-ing these and other skills were considered necessary prerequisites to successful employment and living. In effect, TE was viewed as a training vehicle to help Fountain House members succeed in their future employment endeavors.

Members on TE assignments were also paid at the regular rate established by the employer. This aspect of compensation was important because it guaranteed that the standards for success that employers set were the same for the member as they would be for any other employee selected for the job. By involving employers as partners in the rehabilitation process and guaranteeing equal pay, Beard replicated a precept that he had learned at Eloise—that the activity be normal. The members would gain assurance and a sense of satisfaction that in learning and meeting the job performance requirements they could do the job as well as anyone despite their illness and that they were ready for their own job.

The TE also allowed members to take a risk on employment without the practical consequences of failure. When most people in the population at large begin their employment career, they go through a period of trial and error. Some jobs they succeed at; others they may get fired from. That is normal. For people with mental illness, many of whom were cheated of this stage of career development by the onset of illness during late adolescence, it was only fair, in Beard's way of thinking, that they be given the same opportunities to try out provisional employment. At Fountain House, taking advantage of the opportunity to try, for people who feel threatened by the prospect of working in independent settings, was viewed as a successful behavior regardless of the tangible results of job regularity or continuity.

Fountain House began acquiring jobs under this project quickly. The first arrangement was with a company headed by Karl Keller, a member of the Fountain House Board.[7] By the end of 1959, twenty-two members had worked on jobs provided by seven different companies. Today the program offers members ninety job placements. TE was never intended as an alternative to having one's own job (independent employment); it was meant to initiate the process for those for whom immediate entry into the job market proved insurmountable. Fountain House has since moved to include a variety of avenues for helping its members achieve employment, from supported employment to its newest venture in member-run businesses and social cooperatives.

In a similar fashion, Fountain House began assisting members with housing, another crucial aspect of their life. Most discharged patients were not married and lived with their families. In some cases, they did return to live with their parents. Mostly, however, particularly after long hospitalizations, returning to their parental home was not possible. Usually, in New York City, the only available option for members was a small, dingy room in a single room occupancy (SRO) hotel where bathrooms were shared by a number of occupants. Without employment and with only their welfare stipends as income, most discharged patients could afford only accommodations like these. Beard was keenly aware of how living in SRO hotels exacerbated the loneliness and isolation common among those with mental illness.

Fountain House responded by extending its reach into the housing market. Board member Hetty Richard was instrumental in starting the program by assuming leases herself and providing supplemental funding for additional expenditures, such as the purchase of furniture. Representatives of Fountain House negotiated with landlords and signed leases for apartments in various locations around the city. Fountain House usually arranged for two members to share an apartment, thus reducing costs and allowing opportunities for members to provide companionship to one another. Each member paid Fountain House half the rent, and Fountain House forwarded the rent to the landlord. Rents in New York City at that time were low enough that this arrangement was feasible. Staff workers and other members visited the apartments and assisted the occupants in managing the affairs of daily life. By 1961, eight such apartments had been acquired, and in that year Fountain House received a foundation grant in support of a proposal to secure an additional twenty apartments.[8] Today Fountain House provides residences to more than five hundred of its members.

By 1960, under John Beard's leadership, the essential framework of Fountain House that exists today was well established. It featured the clubhouse with its workday and after-hours programs, and the bridges into the larger society through its employment and housing programs. Each component was, and remains, integral to the others

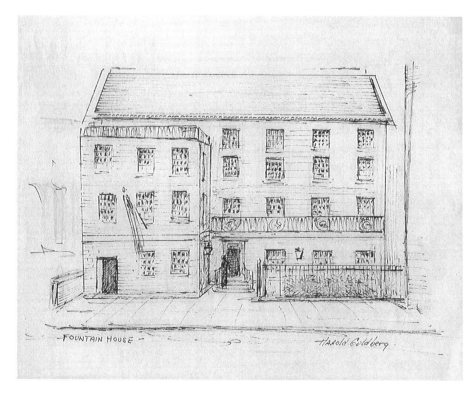

Early member sketch of the new Fountain House (1965)

within the context of a typical work group setting. Over time, Fountain House moved to its current location, across the street from the original building.

As membership and organizational demands increased, additional activity work groups, now called units, were added. Today members and staff collaborate on research, training, a wellness center, education, horticulture, full-time employment, intake, and orientation. Fountain House also incorporates a number of other work areas such as accounting, fund-raising, human resources, and maintenance, which sustain its administration as an independent social agency. Special in-house projects have been created: one is devoted to members who are deaf, another to young adults with mental illness, and another to member advocacy. While administrative work areas are frequently driven by external demands (such as a year-end budget deadline or a fund-raising event), rather than the immediate needs of members, the ongoing processes are open to the members and create opportunities for member responsibility and contribution in greater depth than they might otherwise enjoy. Fountain House has expanded its scope to include an international training institute and a member art gallery. Finally, members and staff are able to gain respite from the city by retreating to High Point, a rural farm in northern New Jersey.

Transforming the Work Environment

There is one final aspect to consider in Beard's swift redesign of Fountain House as a normal regimen of work and recreation. The hardest part of his job at Eloise, and that which commanded his ultimate ingenuity, was how to motivate his patients to step out from their isolation and engage in ordinary group activities. Beard achieved this by tapping into their interests (which he was eminently resourceful at) and awaiting the moment for their active involvement. The move from individual activity or task groups to the whole theater of a work environment offered by Fountain House broadened the potential for motivation from a focus on a lone therapist to the entire social network of talents and imagination of staff and members. At Fountain House, the interests and needs of the group both individually and collectively created a field rife with urgency and opportunity for meaningful engagement. Fountain House essentially achieved the goal of milieu therapy, although in a secularized format, by harnessing all who worked in the immediate area, both members and staff, to reach out and invite members to join in with house operations. It was as if Beard found himself as a lone painter whose modest canvas had been expanded to include a huge wall mural that would employ any number of artists.

The shift in approach from the one-on-one interest of an individual therapist in his clients to the whole social canvas of activities as an ordinary workday environment required one last step, however. If Fountain House was to achieve the recovery outcomes for people living with mental illness as promised in AGT, it had to make sure that those structures that inhibit individuals with mental illness in taking on challenges that are found in general society did not pervade Fountain House. In this respect, the hierarchical arrangement of management and labor with staff employees in the kind of controlling roles that typically govern relationships in work endeavors, including those in mental health agencies, did not appear to Beard to be conducive to the values of choice and collaboration that he envisioned governing relationships at Fountain House. Ultimately, for this population, whose illness typically involved a sense of personal failure and loss of self-confidence (brought on by a pervasive societal stigma toward people with a psychiatric diagnosis as well as self-stigma) and whose anxiety deeply mitigated against their ability to move on with their lives and achieve recovery, Beard would establish a place that guaranteed that the members would always have a seat at the table. He completely transformed all that happened within Fountain House into a humane working community, where all the participants worked with each other in servicing member needs and in running the house. In that process Beard called for a shift in the power arrangements between the professionals and their clients and a new definition of organizational roles that was rarely, if ever, found in other mental health settings. Ultimately, Beard shifted in his thinking from personally motivating people to join in small, disparate, busy groups to forming a community of interests in which the need for member responsibility and contributions—the *need to be needed*—was to become the catalytic operational principle.

3

CORE PRINCIPLES
OF A WORKING COMMUNITY

I say, yes: people need to be needed. And, if doesn't
happen naturally, it's up to some of us to figure out
legitimate ways, that aren't going to be exploitative,
where the individual is needed.

—JOHN BEARD

From its beginnings, Fountain House presented a different approach to aid in psychiatric recovery than its contemporaries did. It underscored this difference by employing special terms to describe itself that were indicative of its inner dynamics. It first adopted "club," for "social club" (Carmichael, 1959), to announce to patients who were leaving mental hospitals what opportunities awaited them on West 47th Street in New York City, in supporting their return to society. Beard frequently used "day program" to refer to the sense of normalcy and doing things that he was introducing at Fountain House through the structure of a workplace during the day followed by social and recreational activities in the evening. One of the most lasting descriptors has been that Fountain House is like a "family." Its popularity is evident from the episode described at the beginning of this book, and it is still commonly used today. Vorspan (2004), for example, at an international congress of clubhouses, while recognizing the limitations of the analogy to a family, nevertheless found it particularly useful in describing the opportunities for personal growth at Fountain House. She explained:

Families are institutions in which different people have different roles and functions. In the family, it is the parent's responsibility to build and maintain a family structure in which children are afforded all kinds of opportunities and resources to attain their highest potential. It is the children's responsibility to make good use of these opportunities and resources as fuel for growth toward their own developing life goals. (p. 27)

Finally, with the publication and wide adoption of the Standards for Clubhouse Programs (Propst, 1992) as the framework for describing the model, the term "work-ordered day" has become typical in highlighting the nature of the contemporary clubhouses that adhere to a Fountain House approach. At the end of his life, John Beard ultimately referred to the essence of Fountain House as an "intentional community" (Beard, Propst, and Malamud, 1982, p. 47) that was purposely designed to provide a restorative environment for severely disabled psychiatric patients. We believe that this last term, *community*, best describes the nature of Fountain House as a unique contemporary therapeutic intervention in mental health.

Why *Community*?

Community is a "relational" term (Cohen, 1985). It is used to distinguish one group from another, or to differentiate a subgroup from the larger society in which it exists. In this respect, communities distinguish themselves from other towns or entities by setting boundaries of one sort or another, sometimes erecting stone markers or even concrete walls. But a community implies more than just proximity; it connotes a relational aspect that goes beyond spatial contiguity. Participating in a community involves how people relate to one another as opposed to those in the outside world (Gusfield, 1975). A community is a place where people congregate as a group and share a sense of identity and relatedness.

Individuals who live in a community experience a sense of belonging with regard to their place in that society and the people with whom they live. Sarason (1974) identified the awareness of relatedness or the feeling of social connectedness that participants in a community experience as the "psychological sense of community." He described the universal human need for and awareness of belonging, intimacy, and usefulness that are normally associated with this concept:[2]

> The community in which we live is a geo-political entity with which we feel little kinship. We may work in the community, pay taxes, and vote, but in no other respect feel a part of it. . . . We do not feel needed in our community and we rarely if ever seriously think about how we can contribute to the solution of its problems. We are busy during the day, tired at night, and seek recreation and entertainment on the weekends. And, if we are parents, there are children who need our attention every day. Where is there time to engage in a community activity? What community activity? What do I have to contribute? Where am I needed? Our lives are circumscribed spatially and psychologically, and it all seems so natural except for those poignant moments, quite frequent for many people, when we yearn to be part of a larger network of relationships that would give greater expression to our needs for intimacy, diversity, usefulness, and belongingness. (pp. 2–3)

Thus community holds both spatial and relational connotations.

It is this rich notion of community as a place that encompasses a relational ethic and one's awareness of being part of a group that is viewed at Fountain House as essential for recovery. Beard understood this. He was acutely aware of the loss of relatedness that resulted from a diagnosis of mental illness. He also understood the instrumental capacities of a community; from his experience at Eloise he knew that task groups as a rudimentary form of community and a setting for supportive relationships were curative. The units or working areas that he formed at Fountain House were also a way of rebuilding the sense of relatedness that most members lacked. As an intentional community, Fountain House offered a way to restore a sense of purpose and vitality to people suffering from mental illness.

Community as an Instrument

Merriam-Webster's Collegiate Dictionary (11th edition) defines the word *community* as "a group of people with a common characteristic or interest living together within a larger society." The core interest or commonality of purpose, its "intentionality," determines the nature of a community, defines its boundaries, and gives meaning and purpose to its constituents. Fountain House holds such an encompassing raison d'être for its various activities. As a community, it is the needs of the membership for psychiatric recovery that define its functional identity. The allied goals of member recovery and social inclusion produce the exigencies for daily activities at Fountain House that fulfill its social mission in meeting the recovery needs of its membership. Its vision statement affirms this goal: "People with mental illness everywhere achieve their potential and are respected as co-workers, neighbors and friends." In effect, Fountain House operates as a recovery community (Whitley, Strickler, & Drake, 2011), wherein its members, despite their illnesses, realize their dreams for recovery.

Such a vision, however, is not limited to Fountain House. Other social service agencies are just as likely to subscribe to a similarly edifying vision of achieving one's potential once outside the hospital (Clay, 2005; Whitley, Strickler, & Drake, 2011). The "process of regaining one's life" (Mancini, Hardiman, & Lawson, 2005) through employment, independent living, and finding a circle of friends broadly represents the new paradigm for organizing recovery efforts for adults with mental illness. While Fountain House holds out the hope for eventual social integration, as a functioning community it is itself an antidote to the social isolation its members experience while living in today's society. Fountain House offers a place that is rich with opportunities for members to determine their personal interests, work on teams, practice making choices and facing the consequences of doing so, and connect with others in realizing the goal of a recovery center. It is through a working community that Fountain House envisions members' regaining their lost connections with their coworkers, family, and friends. Or, as Cohen (1985) has observed, "Community . . . is where one learns and continues to practice how to 'be social'" (p. 15). In sum, community for Fountain House represents both an inspirational ideal (a goal to strive for) and an instrumental methodology (a model for how to attain it). Community is the therapy of Fountain House; it is through a community of members, staff, and volunteers that Fountain House exercises its potency. A number of recent studies of clubhouses reflective of the Fountain House approach confirm the importance of the role that social networks engendered by these places play in overcoming the sense of isolation experienced by members suffering from mental illness (Carolan et al., 2011; Norman, 2006; Pernice-Duca & Onaga, 2009; Waegemakers et al., 2008). The community of Fountain House, therefore, is a place for members to overcome the isolation brought on by the onset of mental illness and to test their wings as social beings as they move on with their lives. Additionally, the appellation *community* applied to Fountain House as a methodology for redressing the social estrangement of its membership points to its unique nature within the constellation of contemporary mental health services. Its design as a *working community* is the singular manner through which it differentiates itself from other social agencies and institutions that similarly embrace recovery and social inclusion as their operational ideal.

The Nature of the Fountain House Working Community

Fountain House has consciously built its community around the social construct of the workplace. Despite its appearance as a workday-like culture, however, there exists an emotional tone to Fountain House that is more than an aggregate of the expectations and practices that have been honed over the years of its focus on being a normal place of work. "Emotional tone" is a nonverbal perception or understanding that is transmitted through the senses. Often, the term is used to describe the atmospheric qualities of music, such as the mood that is communicated through background music in a tense or romantic movie. Members sense the tone of Fountain House, for example, from the first moment they walk through its front doors. When new members enter Fountain House, many express surprise. The comments of one were captured on tape (Anderson, 2005) as she first viewed Fountain House: "And when I came, I mean, I was really shocked. I mean, I did not expect what I saw." The building's appearance made a simple but profound statement of respect to the member. To this prospective member, Fountain House projected a refined appearance, even an affluence, that many of its members lack, or even feel that they do not deserve, in their personal lives. At the very least, it is not what one expects upon entering a mental health clinic.

But more important to new members is how they are received at Fountain House. Every new member is greeted personally when he or she walks through the doors and is given a house tour. During their orientation, new members are expected to make choices and are asked to which unit in the house they'd like to belong, and who they'd like their staff worker to be. These are not the questions mental health patients entering a treatment center for the first time are accustomed to hearing. Fountain House is not a service center where consumers come to access resources to resolve their needs or issues. Fountain House is first and foremost a recovery enterprise where the contributions of members are critical. Therefore, new members are greeted not as illnesses in need of treatment, but as people who can contribute to the common enterprise. Members affirm the importance of such a reception in a comment repeated over and over that is direct and simply stated: "I cover the phones in my unit and greet visitors. Being needed to help in the unit gives me a reason to get up and get going in the morning" (quoted in Jackson, 2001, p. 57). The Fountain House community is intentionally designed as a workplace where people with mental illness participate and make indispensable contributions. Additionally, the humanity and mutuality among members and staff that accompany the flow of the routine activities create a social atmosphere or an emotional tone for the organization that typifies its construction as a working community. And it is the nature of the relationships among those involved in the enterprise, as a community, that forms the core of the Fountain House approach.

The Fountain House working community emanates from the daily application of several core principles that govern the nature of mem-

ber and staff relationships. Specifically, the need for member involvement, the *need to be needed*, member *choice* in all matters, and the
collaborative nature of the human interaction involved constitute a set
of practice principles that imbue Fountain House with a clear workplace cultural identity. These principles set a tone of mutual respect
and productivity that is evident in the exchanges that transpire among
members and staff and that contribute the emotional punch that is evident to anyone who visits. The application of these principles makes
work at Fountain House primarily a relational undertaking. They define the roles that participants assume in carrying out their tasks and
the nature of the personal exchanges that occur. Thus the emotional
tone of Fountain House as a working community—the emotional
tone that Beard spent his entire life fashioning, that new members
and visitors alike sense in the effortless flow of the community—is
based on the practical application of these several core principles that
infuse the quality of the social exchanges among members and staff
with humanity, warmth, animation, and hustle. They create an emotional congruence, a good feeling about how one is being treated,
among the members, which invites their participation and encourages
them to voluntarily assume joint responsibility for the operations of
the house. They provide the justification and meaning of the historical
beliefs, standards, expectations, and practices that have evolved over
the years. Additionally, the nature of the relationships among those
involved in the social enterprise that is Fountain House, its quality
of social exchange, and the underlying principles are what separates
Fountain House from other mental health agencies and challenges society at large in its treatment of people suffering from mental illness.
The remainder of this chapter will clarify the nature of these principles
and discuss their dynamics as humane, strengths-based, voluntary,
and collaborative endeavors, and the outcomes they are projected to
effect as a working community with a manifest purpose in the social
welfare of its clients.

The Need to Be Needed

The *need to be needed* is a central principle in the formation of Fountain House as a working community. It is the spark that ignites the engine of this productive enterprise of intentions and interests impatient for supporting members' resiliency and their achievement of social welfare. As Lanoil once summed up for a new staff worker who inquired about his responsibilities at Fountain House, "The single most significant way that Fountain House can provide rehabilitation for a member is for him to experience being needed" (as quoted in Anderson, 1985). Others have learned, as we have, that when a community offers opportunities for work that is real and meaningful, and the individuals involved accept the invitation freely and make a contribution that is recognized as such, they appear to gain in purposefulness and take on identities indicative of recovery (Mancini, 2006). These studies demonstrate that meaningful, responsible involvement provides people living with mental illness with a renewed "identity marked by competence, agency and wellbeing" (p. 21) that traditional medical model approaches, which are fixated on the illness, tend to neglect. As one member of Fountain House has insightfully written: "To be needed means more to me than anything else in my life, and it also means that I am living a meaningful life. I share many responsibilities with others and, when I don't come in, it's nice to know I'm missed" (Peckoff, 1992). That she was missed was reason enough to motivate her to take up a useful role in the group. Whereas receiving help in many mental health settings (however well intentioned) can engender a feeling of helplessness, an environment where members are asked to contribute their talents is an experience most members have not had since before the onset of their illness. It confers dignity, facilitates basic acceptance, and genuinely invites the members at Fountain House to join in its daily undertakings.

Operationally, the need to be needed structures all house activities in such a way that member participation is required to accomplish the work at hand. A low staff-to-member ratio means that member participation is an essential programmatic reality. Since the number of staff is inadequate to do the work of the house, staff must look to members for help in completing any tasks at hand. Every morning, staff workers face a void that they are incapable of bridging without the assistance of the members. Staff purposely allot space for members in the operation of the house and call on them to take on vital and meaningful roles that have consequences for both their own and others' psychiatric rehabilitation. When Fountain House and its collaborators around the world first formulated the standards for clubhouse programs, they succinctly summarized this practice: "Clubhouse staff are sufficient to engage the membership, yet few enough to make carrying out their responsibilities impossible without member involvement" (International Center for Clubhouse Development, 2012).

This unique dynamic of the need to be needed pervades the environment broadly defined as the Fountain House culture. It flips the normal directionality in the relationships among staff and members from one in which the client needs the staff worker, who possesses some special knowledge or skill (that of a traditional mental health treatment), to one in which it is the staff worker who needs the member's help. It regulates the behavior of staff workers toward the membership, since they must display respect for members for their potential contributions to the enterprise. The need to be needed demands open communications among all the participants and prohibits segregated member or staff space and private member or staff meetings regarding house programming. Thus, in theory as well as in practice, Fountain House members are genuinely needed in every aspect of the operations and there is no house activity from which members can be excluded. It is exactly what John Beard envisioned in establishing Fountain House and modeling it after the tenets of AGT. The need to be needed is infused into the social enterprise that is Fountain House, wherein members become active creators of the community and its purposes, and the workday becomes a natural motivator and instrument to attract member involvement. With the need to be needed, Beard, in effect, transformed a place of work into a working community.

Members as Social Beings

In Beard's day, the formation of such an environment in which it was impossible for the enterprise to exist without the active participation of its membership was novel, but not untried. His strategy reflected a similar approach attempted by contemporary practitioners of therapeutic communities in England (Jones, 1953; Whiteley, 2004) in which the patients were invited to become active contributors to their rehabilitation. More recently, mental health advocates have advanced the value of peer-run interventions related to employment, housing, and illness self-management (Whitley et al., 2007; Whitley, Strickler, & Drake, 2011). And Mandiberg (2010) has enumerated instances in which an enclave or sub-community strategy that fosters participant involvement and ownership has been used to provide support for housing and employment, as well as other social inclusion strategies on behalf of people suffering from mental illness. All these strategies together ground their claims to effectiveness in the existence of an inherent dimension of human nature, the primacy of the human being as a social being.

The need to be needed appeals to the notion of *relatedness* that long has been accepted as an innate dimension of human nature, one of several enduring motivators of human behavior (Maslow, 1954). The notion of belonging or relatedness stands among the elementary drives of human nature (as, for example, the physiological need for food, drink, and shelter or the growth needs for self-actualization and self-esteem) that act on a vital level of human development and motivation (Alderfer, 1972). By appealing to the personal sense of usefulness within the group—at Fountain House a member cannot belong to a group without knowing that his or her presence is needed by the group—Fountain House expands on the notion of relatedness and fuses it with a complementary need for self-actualization. The need to be needed therefore recognizes the vital importance a person places on being accepted as a contributing member of a group. It sets up an environment where the member is going to be treated as a person with capabilities and not as an illness to be cured. Thus, the need to be needed establishes a first step in constructing a working community—namely, the organizational opening for participation and the structural invitation to join in. Relying on a distinct human awareness that constitutes a universal and essential ingredient for human growth and development, the need to be needed presents a pervasive structure within Fountain House that appeals to areas of health and vitality, which remain unaffected by mental illness, to engage the members in the work of the day.

Moreover, the application of the need to be needed is similar to concepts and techniques employed by major humanistic thought of the twentieth century concerned with personal motivation and development. Rogers (1961), for example, stated that in achieving the good life and becoming a fully functioning human being the individual also "discovers that he is soundly and realistically social" (p. 192). Fromm (1956) eloquently described the deepest need of man as the need "to overcome his separateness, to leave the prison of his aloneness" (p. 9). Deci (1995) acknowledges the notion of "connectedness" as an essential human need and determinant in understanding human motivation and behavior. McMillan and Chavis (1986) consider the need that people feel to exert influence in the group as one of the four constituent elements of experiencing a sense of community. In organizing its daily activities around the principle of the need to be needed, Fountain House has developed a treatment for people who have been stripped of human dignity and made to feel a stranger in their community. Its application is intended to engage members at a vital level and re-ignite their connection to ordinary human endeavors. And, as we shall discuss later, it has embedded within the working community a wholly unique way of working between professionals and their clients in the mental health and social work fields.

Furthermore, in appealing to an innate human need that applies regardless of culture, the concept of the need to be needed establishes Fountain House as a robust model for widespread, even international replication. While establishing itself as a local, living social enterprise, Fountain House is not tethered to its moorings in New York City. It is more than a place; it represents an idea of hope for people with mental illness that transcends its locality. And, in operationalizing itself as a working community driven by the principle of the need to be needed among its members, Fountain House broadcasts daily an expansive vision of how people with mental illness can live and work in any everyday society. The principle of the need to be needed and its resulting working community practice that captures the social essence of being human are applicable to people living with mental illness worldwide.

For such a system to work practically, however, two ancillary conditions are necessary. First, Beard realized that his appeal for member participation in group activities had to be wholly voluntary and free of any hint of external rewards or constraints. Fountain House in this respect had to appeal to the internal motivation of its membership. Second, since the need to be needed radically transformed the dynamics of routine staff–client relationships, the professional role of staff worker had to be redefined from one based on hierarchy, specialization, and deficit-based treatment approaches to one based on client strengths and collaboration. Together, the need to be needed, member choice, and a collaborative staff role become supports of a three-legged stool that forms the inner DNA of Fountain House and any clubhouse that adopts its approach.

Choice

At Fountain House, a symbiotic relationship exists between member choice and the need to be needed. Member choice is an ethical and instrumental practice that flows logically throughout an organization that espouses member employment as a direct outcome. When staff workers face demanding workloads (recall that a working community is purposely understaffed), they may unwittingly lose focus and become overly concerned about organizational productivity—lunch has to be served; plants have to be watered; reports have to be published. Staff workers can easily become distracted from their responsibility to create a supportive environment for member recovery. Thus, without member choice, the need to be needed could easily slip into the exploitation of individuals without compensation for their services. Member choice serves as the brake, the means of avoiding such a collision. It thwarts the possibility of exploitation of members as unpaid labor. It challenges agencies that purport to be following the Fountain House model but use understaffing as a cost-cutting measure rather than an empowerment device. Such agencies allow themselves to become so short-staffed, or so dependent on specific members' contributions, that they may interrupt members' progress toward achieving their life goals (Vorspan, 2004). They make work an end in itself.

Beard (1978), on the other hand, knew from his experience with AGT that accommodating members' "readiness" was a necessary precondition for their being capable of acting normally and responsibly. He recognized that for recovery to take place he "had to have some way of trying to pursue this issue of personal freedom" (p. 13) whereby members were given room to take responsibility for their actions. He viewed work, therefore, as a means to an end, a tool in the hands of skilled staff to foster the recovery of the members. And, in an environment that subscribes to the notion that members are capable of acting on their own behalf, room must be left for individuals to assume responsibility for their actions. This is accomplished through choice.

The power "to carve out your own future" or "ride your own horse" (Beard, 1978) embodies exciting prospects that are well supported by empirical evidence (Baylis, 2004; Gardner, 1997; Howe, 1990). Similarly, studies within the mental health consumer movement demonstrate how coercion, or the lack of choice, ranks as "the most detrimental factor to the recovery process" (Mancini, 2006, p. 21). Members at Fountain House readily admit that the sense of autonomy and self-efficacy that they gain from participation in the Fountain House community has a lot more motivational pull than cash stipends for attendance. Deciding how and when to become involved in an activity (rather than receiving extrinsic rewards) becomes the source of internal motivation for member participation in a workday situation at Fountain House.

This should come as no surprise. Choice contributes to the intrinsic sense of personal autonomy or self-determination, and self-determination and empowerment are vital for success in recovery (Chamberlin, Rogers, & Edison, 1996). The experience of Fountain

House corroborates years of research by Deci and Ryan (1985) into how self-determination and autonomy arise from the self-motivational effects of choice. Deci (1995) has noted that "self motivation, rather than external motivation, is at the heart of creativity, responsibility, healthy behavior, and lasting change" (p. 9). These are the same positive programmatic outcomes that result from the voluntary participation by members at Fountain House.

At Fountain House, freedom of choice in all matters guarantees that members can decide what days they will attend Fountain House and what days they will spend doing other things. Once members have arrived, choice presides over the activities they engage in, the staff with whom they work, their pace and degree of involvement, and when they will call it a day and leave. Throughout Fountain House, choice is a mechanism for member empowerment. Furthermore, choice, when combined with organizational goal planning and members' involvement in organizational decision making, inculcates a pride of ownership among the membership and suffuses the operations with a sense of fairness. This is an important issue in a voluntary organization such as Fountain House. As Chua and Iyengar (2006) emphasized, when people have choices, they have a sense of personal control and empowerment that facilitates their motivation to participate. It offers members the opportunity to take charge of their lives, wresting the responsibility for their recovery from the mental health experts and putting it in their own hands. In effect, authentic member choice is how Fountain House operationalizes the popular cry of today's consumer movement: "Nothing about us without us." It transforms a popular slogan into a programmatic ingredient in the recovery process.

Finally, the right of members to choose for themselves attracts participation without the co-option of the sense of autonomy and personal responsibility, which can occur in helping programs. In creating an environment composed of work that needs both attention and choice, Fountain House resolves the dilemma that many social workers face in attempting to help people in need within the regimen of a hierarchical organization. Hierarchical differentials that operate in professional helping situations such as mental health facilities, in which staff, who are trained as experts, are eager to assist their clients, who face real-life problems, can undermine the sense of autonomy and self-efficacy that we and others believe is so important for re-covery. Deci (1995) describes the dilemma that mental health staff workers typically face:

> How can people in one-up positions, such as health care providers or teachers, motivate others, such as their patients or students who are in one-down positions, if the most powerful motivation, lead-ing to the most responsible behavior, must come from within—if it must be internal to the self of the people in the one-down positions? (p. 10)

At Fountain House, the right of member choice in all dealings off-sets this imbalance and places the agency of recovery squarely in the hands of members. Imitators, who lack a full understanding of the working community model, miss the critical notion that staff must cede the initiative to the member. Consequently, choice calls for a change in staff as well as in members, in which staff adjust their pro-fessional demeanor to become that of a colleague and facilitator.

Professional Orientation as Colleagues

If the need to be needed is the spark that triggers the engine of Fountain House as a working community, and choice is the key that turns on its ignition (a key that is held by members), then the actions of staff are the oil that keeps the house running smoothly. The entire operation of Fountain House is designed as a collaborative effort among members, staff, and volunteers. This insistence of a staff–member collabora-tive approach dates back to Beard's experience on the ward at Eloise. Beard and his colleagues found that the quality of the member–staff relationship there colored the social exchanges involved and actively contributed to member empowerment and recovery. Beard (1978) saw that the "we" (the staff workers) and the "they" (the patients) needed to be engaged on an equal basis for progress in recovery to take place.

He realized that if he could offset the hierarchical imbalance inherent in the provider–patient model and replace it with the desire for member contributions and involvement, the power differential in any provider–patient relationship could actually have a positive impact. In fact, what makes Fountain House work on a day-to-day operational level is the strength of this redesigned relationship between its members and its staff. Beard explained his therapeutic insight as follows:

> A lot of this was going on in those years of trying to get more of a total push.[3] Because, what else did you have? I'm sure I could go on with a lot of further examples, but . . . what we were doing is saying that this chronic patient is capable of doing more things than what he is doing on the ward. And that if you get the patient doing those things, he would begin to be perceived differently. And when you're perceived differently, you will be treated differently. You might get a little more words like: "Thank you." Or, "Hey, that's good." Or, "Would you like to?" And that's all we had at our disposal. (p. 7)

Consequently, Fountain House has structurally realigned the member–staff relationship from a hierarchical to a collaborative approach. The exchanges that take place in such settings—the expression by staff workers of the need for member contributions and their personal expressions of confidence, support, and appreciation—alter the members' sense of themselves and their capabilities. With staff encouragement, members gain in trust and see themselves not as problems but as solutions to problems, which in turn builds up their self-confidence. On an individual level, members become emboldened to take progressively longer strides on their road to recovery. Vorspan (2000) describes how this aspect of the Fountain House working community supports member recovery:

> Mental illness robs people of their identities, their sense of self, and of the meaning in their lives. We begin the process of rediscovering who we are when someone looks us in the eye and says, "I need you." If and when we are genuinely addressed this way, we begin to accept, even if only in the most tentative and tiny way, that here

is actually still a "me" to be needed by another person. And then, when we step out to meet that need, and agree to engage in whatever the work is, we have no choice but to acknowledge that "I am, still." That though broken, I still *am*, and that by working together with this other person, I seem to grow, ever so slowly stronger. (p. 35)

So, by fashioning a social context in which the natural power relationships are rearranged—where member participation is needed and expected, and member choice is respected, Fountain House changes the way people with mental illness think about themselves, which in turn motivates member participation.

In effect, Fountain House exploits the natural power discrepancy in the member–staff relationship to create positive outcomes in the lives of its members. Whereas clients elsewhere ask the experts for help, professional staff at Fountain House are dependent on members for the successful accomplishment of their house assignments. They must regularly initiate contact with members, ask them for their help, and show appreciation for the contributions members make to the group. And since members participate voluntarily, staff workers must continually fine-tune these relationships—developing the confidence to be able to acknowledge their own limitations in situations and having the humility to recognize a member who takes responsibility as a colleague. In this way, the staff role at Fountain House shifts the normal axis of power in the staff–client framework from a hierarchical to a collegial plane. Fountain House is a prime example of the future of exemplary practice in social work—a strengths-based (as opposed to a deficit-centered) approach in which staff see members as valuable contributors in their recovery process (Rapp & Goscha, 2006; Saleebey, 1992), rather than as people who need help with their problems. The strengths-based perspective is an instrument for empowerment in which those with status share with those without. As a staff person at Fountain House has been overheard to say, aptly describing the staff role: "Every day you walk into work, you bring with you a bag filled with power. Your job is to empty it before you leave."

Unique Organizational Design

While each of the strategies described above represents nothing new in mental health treatment, organizing mental health practice as a community effort of members and staff within design features that promote occupational activities, collegiality, and choice does establish a new way of working. An environment where staff need members (i.e., where understaffing is purposeful), and members have choice as to how they will participate in the organization, requires a different organizational platform than what is commonly called for in today's mental health facilities—as a community effort in recovery rather than one that is organized to deliver individualized services. Fountain House controls its spaces in such a way as to foster this impact. Fountain House favors open spaces for group activities to occur (as opposed to small offices or cubicles where individual staff meet one on one with their clients to conduct case management or counseling). Spatially it exemplifies a communal structure in which members and

The open spaces of the clerical unit facilitate task-group activities.

staff respond jointly to common needs and interests of the member-ship. It opts for a more fluid design, where client voluntarism can flourish and groups of members and staff can loosely form and recon-stitute themselves as the needs of the moment require. This is not to say that Fountain House does not address individual needs. Rather, it organizes them in a different manner than the traditional community mental health center does. Member acceptance and intake at Fountain House, for example, are expressive of an organizational design that supports a communal approach to receiving personal services.

New Member Intake

Member acceptance by Fountain House underscores its unconditional commitment to adults suffering from mental illness—the sole eligibil-ity requirement is being an adult with a mental illness. Offering recov-ery services with little or no selectivity of its membership is relatively unique organizationally. Staff do not conduct level-of-readiness tests. They serve all adults with mental illness without distinction (accepting them primarily as people, not as people with problems). Once mem-bers are admitted on the basis of a diagnosis of serious mental illness,[4] they are not farmed out to the specific services the agency considers applicable. They are treated like people capable of making contribu-tions (not like people with specific flaws in need of repair) and are given immediate access to any activities and services that they choose as full members of a living, working community.

Concurrently, Fountain House staff workers are not constrained to work with their clients in the categories that typically structure social work agencies, such as individual or group counseling, classes in activities of daily living, case management, or housing or employ-ment information offices. Since staff workers at Fountain House need the members in order to fulfill their own responsibilities, they cannot approach members solely in terms of their expertise or specialties. They must eschew any functional fixedness that reflects a departmen-talized service delivery system. Rather, staff present themselves as open to a wide range of individual member needs and interests. On any given day, staff work with members one on one, in small work groups, or on a macro level with other social agencies on member rights and benefits. As explained by Dougherty (1994), staff workers wear multiple hats—for example, as managers and educators on the unit, or as advocates in disputes with government bureaucracies about member benefits. Staff workers at Fountain House are expected to be highly skilled professionals capable of engaging with members through a strengths-based approach to practice. In sum, the expectations for staff are consistent with the diversity of skills and flexibility of thought reflected by a generalist practitioner in social work (Jackson et al., 1996; Locke, Garrison, & Winship, 1998). Within the field of social work, a generalist extracts values and practices common to the specialty roles in social work and employs them as he or she sees fit to support their constituent principles and techniques in various practice settings. Here, "role flexibility" is a defining characteristic (Etzioni, 1961, p. 320; Kirst-Ashman, 2010, p. 95).

Fountain House staff must be flexible; in fact, they must be radically so. Their outreach to members is characterized as that of generalists who are open to communicating with members on any number of diverse issues. In addition to participating in a normal work atmosphere, Fountain House staff workers are expected to engage with members in an unlimited range of everyday situations. They are asked to relate to members professionally at a workplace and socially after hours. And finally, in a significant departure from traditional social work practice as discussed in chapter 6 on motivational coaching, Fountain House staff workers are expected throughout to form authentic, influential, and significant relationships with members.

Organizational Paradigms Compared

Fountain House calls for a redesign of how mental health agencies organize the delivery of their services from an individualized to a communal service purveyor. It transforms the role and expectations of staff who work within the organization to those that value teamwork over hierarchy, choice over compliance, and real work rather than

TABLE 3.1
Professional Organization Paradigm Shift

	Community Mental Health Model	Working Community Model
Organizational Principle	Hierarchy	Teamwork
Approach	Deficit-based	Strengths-based
	Diagnostic	Motivational
	Specialist	Generalist
Environment	Simulated	Real
Expertise/Skill Base	Pedagogical	Relational
	Awareness-oriented	Task-oriented
	Solver	Enabler
	Individualized treatment	Social practice

educational or simulated treatments. As a result, Fountain House staff are expected to approach their work from a strengths-based perspective that is more motivational than diagnostic in design and as generalists who are flexible in understanding the boundaries of the work with their clients (and not inhibited by a specialist definition of professional expertise). Staff are skilled in relational techniques that focus on enabling and empowering members in real-life situations rather than those that posit staff as experts providing solutions. Ultimately, the difference lies in the provision of the craft of social practice (see part II of this book) over specialized treatments.

A relationship that demands that staff workers meet members on a variety of levels is a challenging job that requires a highly skilled level of interpersonal proficiencies. We equate it to the professional profile expected of a general manager in a business: the manager must demonstrate a versatility of interpersonal skills and understandings across multiple situations and disciplines. Consequently, while Fountain House has historically hired staff from a diversity of backgrounds, in recent years only applicants who hold master's degrees have been accepted.[5] The goal in looking for staff is to find someone who maintains a positive attitude in the potential of members while working in seemingly chaotic environments with multiple participants. Additionally, as the diverse demands upon the generalist staff worker challenge staff to dig deep within their own personalities to extract creative and genuine solutions in their exchanges with members, it is essential that they develop their own charisma.

Charisma is the influence that one person exerts on the understanding or behavior of another. It is not based on external attributes such as one's status in a hierarchical organization, but instead on an inherent mix of personal qualities or use of self and personal judgment that social workers are routinely expected to demonstrate. Fountain House expects its staff workers to develop a sense of personal charisma. In fact, successful Fountain House staff workers are exemplars of effective social practice. As Etzioni (1961) noted, normative organizations, as Fountain House could be classified,[6] "are noted for their effectiveness when charisma is broadly represented, especially at the level of direct service providers" (p. 320). Fountain House demonstrates the validity of Etzioni's observation in its more than sixty-year history of social work practice with its highly versatile and skilled professional staff workers who take on collaborative as well as charismatic roles in the organization. For Fountain House, then, the relationship between staff workers and members finds its professional definition outside of today's predominant bureaucratic medical model.

A Note on Place

Finally, a working community assumes place. Location and space are the necessary prerequisites of an association where face-to-face collaboration among participants is paramount. Beard intuitively understood the imperative of having a place of one's own for his vision to materialize. Because the conditions he envisioned differed so radically from the culture and practices of the hospital ward with its fixation on illness, he located an empty storeroom in Eloise as a "place" where he and his patients were free to set up a social space that would relate to the healthy interests of his patients and enable him to pursue what amounted to a different role as therapist. Ultimately he knew that the hospital environment was limited. So when the opportunity presented itself to build his own program at Fountain House, he took it.

It is critically important to people suffering from mental illness to have a place for association in society (Carolan et al., 2011; Whitley, Strickler, & Drake, 2011). The notion of place holds an existential quality, such that the associations that occur within that space become rich in meaning and memory. Relph (1976) has called places "important sources of individual and communal identity" (p. 141). Place then represents a welcome harbor for a population whose *place* in society is filled with stigma and embarrassment. Since deinstitutionalization and the loss of a special place for people suffering from mental illnesses—however ill-conceived and experienced—Fountain House represents one such niche where they can anchor to find meaning and stability and foster relationships with others.

Place can also have a salutary effect upon people. In the words of Ryden (1993), "A sense of place can therefore sustain identity; provide connections to a personal and collective past, offering an emotional center. It is a rooted and anchored locus of meaning and value" (p. 95). In this way, having a place to go to, with its bonds of emotional and social supports, provides a pathway for negotiating the complexities of living for those who still feel homeless and without roots while still living in society (Casey, 1993). March et al. (2008), analyzing place and its association with the etiology of severe mental illness, consider place to function as a reservoir of risk or resilience: "As a reservoir, place consists of the natural and built environment, physical structures, and material resources that shape experience within a designated geographic location. The physical and social architecture of place both shapes and reflects relationships among individual inhabitants, social groups and social structures and institutions" (p. 96). We agree that the social processes found in a place can be both protective and curative for those stricken with mental illness. And we intend to pursue this line of thought in further detail in the afterword, considering how the place Fountain House as a practice and message of hope can provide clues that assist in the amelioration of the problems faced by people with severe mental illness in an era of deinstitutionalization.

Finally, control over space and time is essential in order to sustain the full effects of the Fountain House approach. We now know, after years of attempts to replicate the experience of Fountain House, that spatial independence is a necessary precondition for the working community model to reach its potential in meeting the recovery goals of its membership. It requires a space uninhibited by the rules and mores of a traditional mental health setting. It requires new roles for members and staff so that they can work together in a sympathetic environment. Specifically, such a place requires an independent board of directors at its core who will work to realize the Fountain House mission of member empowerment over the long term. In their own building with their own name, and with an unlimited future, independent working communities can foster a message of hope and demonstrate a sustainable approach to recovery.

In summary, the working community that is Fountain House is a living, humane, strengths-based, voluntaristic, and collaborative endeavor that instills hope in its membership through its commitment to social justice and sensitivity to the struggle for a decent human existence posed by mental illness. To achieve its goals, Fountain House transforms major (yet normal) aspects of human life—daily work and social recreation—into an engine for social welfare for people living with mental illness by establishing the need to be needed, member choice, and a collaborative staff–client professional model within normal task-group methodologies. Part II of this book explores the strategies and techniques by which staff and others at Fountain House create a working community—namely, the professional application of *social practice.*

PART II

Social Practice

4

DEFINING
SOCIAL PRACTICE

Fountain House acts as a prosthetic for members to reestablish
their lives in the community.

—JOHN BEARD

Staff workers at Fountain House, like practitioners everywhere, come
to work thinking about what they have to accomplish that day. On
Tuesdays, staff working in the horticulture unit know that they have
to purchase fresh flowers for the house. If the meat order failed to
arrive the previous day, then those working in the kitchen have to
rethink a lunch menu that was otherwise planned. Materials may need
to be copied in the clerical unit for an upcoming job fair. In the employment unit, staff who are scheduled to accompany members to an
employment office must decide which tasks need to be taken care of
before leaving and which can be postponed for another day. Whatever
the needs for the day, staff workers anticipate their responsibilities
and plan how to accomplish them.

Fountain House, however, is not an ordinary place of business that
organizes daily tasks to achieve productive ends. At Fountain House,
work is not an end in itself. Work is a means to an end and a framework for the recovery of the members suffering from mental illness.
Although Fountain House may not look like a mental health facility,
staff workers know that the manner in which they go about their daily
tasks has a profound impact upon members' lives and their recover-
ies. Consequently, staff workers at Fountain House are expected to

augment their work routines by infusing their pending responsibilities with an additional layer of consideration regarding the organization of the workday and the quality of their relationships with members that the work engenders. Fountain House as a working community must become an invitation that solicits member involvement. Members must sense that their participation is needed, and they must be given the opportunity to contribute something of themselves that is meaningful and valued by the organization. In this way, the organization as a working community is designed to be a tool for staff in making Fountain House a humane, meaningful, socially binding, and productive experience for members.

John Beard once described the functioning of Fountain House as creating "prosthetics" for members to reestablish their lives in the community. To accomplish their goals, staff workers are expected to view the tasks of the day not just as activities to be organized or work to get done, but more importantly as occasions for members to become true collaborators and contributors in the work of the house. Daily, staff workers at Fountain House are asked to rephrase the question "What am *I* going to do today?" to "What must *we* do today?" or "How can I offer members a genuine part to play in the day's agenda?" It is a daunting undertaking, commonly referred to as working "side by side."

Such intentionality in the staff role is not always evident to outsiders visiting the Fountain House community. Visitors see people absorbed in various activities; participants appear to be autonomous and move about without much obvious direction. Absent are the trappings that distinguish the professional from the client, which are common in most mental health facilities. There is virtually no mark or insignia to distinguish staff from members; there are no staff uniforms or badges, no separate offices or "staff only" lunchrooms or bathrooms. This is deliberate. John Beard did not define Fountain House as just a place of work. Rather, the organizational framework (the "day program," as he referred to it) was intended as a means for staff to forge the day's work into a meaningful and relationally supportive environment where members feel valued and where they can become contributing participants in a common enterprise. Beard once clarified this point for a film producer who was puzzled by what he observed taking place at Fountain House:

> Most of all, Fountain House is a process. It's a social process and our job is to single out what is going on. The answer does not lie in the fact that people are in the kitchen. It does not lie that people are up in the snack bar or in the clerical office or are around the house cleaning. That's not the answer—making a repair or painting the walls. That's merely the situation they are in. The process . . . is related to the fact that the patient who comes to our doors has something to offer. Second we have a need for that. We can utilize it. We prize it and we value it. This is what enables the patient, therefore, to participate and undergo the experience—that he's needed. That he does have some self-esteem because we have esteem for him. This is the process we are trying to develop. (Propst, 1967, reel 13, track 40)

Simply engaging in concrete activities of a workday is not what transforms members' lives at Fountain House. Rather, it is the contributions made by members combined with a quality of exchange and the recognition that accompanies the completion of these processes. Vorspan (2000), an insightful writer about clubhouse matters, explained how the Fountain House approach plays out in the interaction of an everyday but real human exchange and dialogue:

> It's not the work in itself that heals. . . . What does heal is the fact that clubhouse staff meet members in the context of needing them. Staff are pushed to look beyond the "shell" the member hides under, and to seek to find the person, no matter how tightly hidden or inaccessible that member has made him or herself. Because there is real, demanding work to be done, the staff has no choice but to try to connect with the place in that member that is vital, healthy, and full of hope whether or not the member recognizes that such a place still exists. (p. 35)

Turning a task into a tool for psychiatric recovery is the principal job demanded of staff workers at Fountain House. It requires staff to manage the space between the indispensable involvement of members in the operation of the house and their autonomy to choose whether and how they will participate. In other words, we view the essential ingredient in supporting member recovery—member engagement in communal activities—as both necessary and voluntary. The framework for solving this challenge is the creation of an opportunity-rich and relationally supportive social ecology. The Fountain House working community is, and must be, inherently welcoming, respectful of choice, meaningful, and strengths-based in order to attract member involvement. The establishment of such a framework requires highly skilled professional expertise: that of the social practitioner. In the chapters that follow, we will explain how one accomplishes this through the "side-by-side" approach pioneered at Fountain House, which we term *social practice*.[1]

Social Practice as a Profession

Fountain House staff social workers share the same means of establishing their credentials and public identity as any other professional class. In commanding respect for the responsibilities they hold, all professional practitioners—whether teachers, engineers, city planners, or social workers—are guided by an innate human ideal and a set of core values combined with a related set of rigorous principles of action and competencies. Similarly, Fountain House staff workers integrate the final causality of their visionary ideals with the efficient technologies that delineate their expertise.

First, social practice at Fountain House is centered on the vision that dominates professional social work practice and animates the energies of its practitioners—namely, the ideal of social justice. Whereas the medical profession is committed to healing, and teachers gain personal satisfaction when they see their students acquire new knowledge and apply it, social workers are energized in their profession by an intense commitment to promoting social justice. Social justice is defined as "an ideal condition in which all members of society have the same rights, protections, opportunities, obligations, and social benefits" (Finn & Jacobson, 2008). It is a principle that social workers list among their core ethical values in the social work Code of Ethics (National Association of Social Workers, 2008). Clearly, it was out of a deep sense of social righteousness that Beard and his early colleagues created Fountain House—they wanted to ensure that its members would not be denied access to meaningful employment, ordinary living settings, or human affiliation, all of which their diagnoses frequently precluded. In this respect, Beard often quoted a maxim he learned from his mother: "Do what has to be done." It is the same commitment to social justice that informs the daily actions of today's Fountain House staff and members.

The term *practice* refers to the repertoire of beliefs, understandings, and methodologies that professionals employ within the domains of their attention, and the kind of solutions their clients can come to expect from them. As social practitioners, Fountain House staff workers must be adept in a host of skills that involve both strategies that foster the social ecology of a working community (such as shared decision making) and relational aptitudes (such as coaching) that sustain members in their quests for personal recovery. At Fountain House, social practice skill sets are further delineated by an adherence to the underlying values of a practical skepticism and innovation that fulfill Schön's (1983) vision of the action-oriented, problem-solving "reflective practitioner."

Attributes of Social Practice

It is important to note that despite the vigorous ethical imperative for social justice, Fountain House staff workers are not ideologues who scrupulously apply established techniques, as if an exact recipe exists for organizing a workday that results in a meaningful and relationally supportive working community. Staff workers grasp that no cookbook solutions exist for the unexpected situations and emergencies that will assuredly arise. This is not to say that theory doesn't inform the performance of social practice. Certainly practice at Fountain House was broadly informed by Beard's original insights from his days at Eloise. At Fountain House, however, concepts are always ancillary to their intended outcomes—the social recovery of Fountain House members. Strategies employed in achieving outcomes are subject to a review and judgment geared toward achieving the desired effect. In this sense, theory is the midwife to practice. It informs the understanding. It opens one to practical possibilities. But it does not dictate those possibilities; they must be validated through experience and research. Ultimately, the house that Beard built was the product of a hands-on social empiricist, not an organizational theorist.

John Beard was clear about this aspect of his work. Whenever he was asked to speak about the nature of Fountain House, he would begin his remarks by inviting a Fountain House member to tell his or her own story. Invariably, the story was about the impact that Fountain House had on the member's ability to turn his or her life around, find employment, and remain out of the hospital. Beard knew that Fountain House had a transformative impact upon its members, and he always wanted his audience to bear in mind that his ultimate objective was the creation of an environment that supported recovery in its members. As a result, he measured everything that occurred at Fountain House against the mission of the social inclusion of the members in society. Beard was, in his heart, a social worker. He described the functioning of Fountain House as creating "prosthetics" for members to reestablish their lives in the community. At Fountain House he sustained only those practices that produced results and had a positive impact on the lives of people living with mental illness.

As social practitioners, intent upon member recovery, staff workers are always open to revision and innovation. Glazer (1974) observed that the profession of social work is marked by ambiguous ends, shifting contexts of practice, and no fixed content of professional knowledge. In a conceptual environment constantly in flux, adaptation and innovation are critical for survival. It takes an inventive mind to maneuver through the minefields of the mental health service system. In this respect, Beard was an eminent social innovator. His signature accomplishment, Fountain House as a working community, still stands today as a model of ingenuity where normal relationships arising out of everyday activities create therapeutic conditions for people suffering with mental illness. Fountain House has continued this tradition of inquiry and inventiveness: the Fountain Gallery was opened as a social cooperative to promote the sale of works produced by Fountain House artists. Through its supported education initiative, the percentage of members attending college and succeeding has grown to more than twice that of the national average for people suffering from mental illness who are attending supported educational programs (Madison & Maltz, 2012).

A final aspect of Beard's legacy is the ongoing expectation that staff will be reflective in their work. Beard regularly submitted the content of his endeavors to review for feedback. As he conceptualized programs and services at Fountain House, he persistently scrutinized their effectiveness as tools for staff to develop meaningful relationships with members. At daily afternoon meetings, Beard would discuss the concepts of acceptance, attention to member strengths (which sidestepped pathology and de-emphasized the past), choice, the creation of successive positive experiences, and rewarding healthy behavior. He had derived these practices from AGT and constantly resubmitted them to others for feedback for their continued or amended application. Staff today continue this practice, employing a homegrown, problem-solving methodology called "best practices."

Fountain House regularly uses roundtable discussion as a forum for instruction and guidance of staff in the performance of their jobs. In a best-practice forum, members and staff meet on a regular basis to address emergent issues or problems of practice. The intention here is to adhere to a contextual pedagogy in which issues are discussed as they naturally arise in the work experience of the staff. The structure offers an opportunity for reflection on practice with ready access to experienced coaches, including the members present, who are expected to provide feedback as well. It should be understood that the solutions to most of the issues that arise are rarely dictated by formal house policies, guidelines, or standards. Rather, their resolution is achieved through the application of insights and commonsense notions, or "best practices," that have been gathered over the years from experienced individuals within the group. Thus, an ongoing direct dialogue between members and staff workers allows for a practical understanding of action to emerge.

Best practices should not be confused with the type of individual-member case meetings found in traditional mental health settings. Rather, the objective of best practices here focuses on the exigencies of real situations as they arise—discussions here involve what the staff is to do, not any decisions or actions to take regarding the behavior of individual members. Best practices thus provide a contextual framework for supporting continuous professional problem solving and developmental growth.

In sum, while staff workers at Fountain House may appear to exercise a different role than is customary in mental health agencies (and one that can be mistakenly characterized as unprofessional, given the mundane nature of its activities), the practice of staff workers at Fountain House retains the essential vision of social work as promoting social justice and requires a challenging regimen of advanced skills and expertise that results in an innovative and reflective performance.

Social Practice Today

Practice at Fountain House has evolved since those early heady days with Beard. While we retain the simple mandate for an essential staff role in the process, we are clearer now on how staff workers engage members in a meaningful and relationally supportive working community. Two generic approaches currently characterize social practice at Fountain House.

The first strategy, transformational design deals with the repertoire of skills and understandings that staff workers employ in transforming the structure of the environment at hand. We call this transformational design because it involves taking the initiative in redesigning the immediate social environment in which the members associate on a daily basis. In effect, Fountain House transforms the standard processes of an ordinary workday into a social environment in which members feel that they have a rightful place and can make a meaningful contribution despite their illnesses. Ultimately, transformational design introduces into the fabric of a workplace a dynamic that promotes member access and empowerment. Additionally, as an extension of this practice, staff at Fountain House seek to eliminate barriers to employment and other forms of social segregation imposed in the broader society as a result of members' illnesses and assist members in utilizing program opportunities outside the Fountain House community in areas such as health maintenance and wellness, education, employment, and social recreation. Transformational design in effect realizes the goal of the recovery movement by redesigning the environment in which members work on a regular basis so that people with mental illness can once again live and thrive in society.

The second strategy, motivational coaching, concerns the manner in which staff form significant, one-on-one relationships with Fountain House members. Motivational coaching involves reaching out to members in isolation and fostering a significant relationship to help them bridge issues arising from risk-taking, fears, and anxiety. Coaching dictates the manner in which this is done so as to respect member agency, dignity, and choice.

In the following chapters, we will discuss each of these approaches and explore situations that call for their application, the attitudes and skills that staff need in performing these interventions, and their intended purpose and outcomes within a recovery paradigm. For now, suffice it to say that all staff at Fountain House are expected to perform both as transformational designers and as motivational coaches. Both functions are integral to employment at Fountain House and form complementary aspects of the staff role. Like having more than one entry to the same room, both are necessary for the job of engaging members in communal activities and in forming a working community that supports member recovery. Individual staff workers may differ, however, in the degree to which they take on these responsibilities.

Line staff working in the units, for example, are expected to function equally, in transformational design through organizing the work of the unit and in motivational coaching through entering into significant, supportive relationships with members. Some staff workers in the units may be better at one aspect of the position than another. For example, there are some staff workers whose expertise, such as a facility with technology or a job developer's access to businesses, allows them to emphasize their functioning in transformational design.

At times these staff may become more involved with planning and explaining the work than with forming extensive one-on-one relationships. But unit staff cannot lack proficiency in either aspect of their dual responsibilities. Administrative staff who work in resource areas such as fund-raising, human resources, or finance, on the other hand, function primarily as transformational designers by promoting access to their spheres of activities or by forming subcommittees or task forces. Given that their training and expertise are not in social work, they perform only minimally as motivational coaches. Thus all staff at Fountain House exercise these principal job functions of transformational design and motivational coaching, though the degrees of intensity may vary from one staff member to another.

Members and Others as Social Practitioners

It is also important to note here that transformational design and motivational coaching are not exclusively staff proficiencies. Anyone in the Fountain House community can acquire and practice skills in these areas. Members in particular take on these responsibilities as a component of their path to recovery. For the purposes of our exposition here, however, the focus is on the role of staff at Fountain House, and, as such, we will refer for the most part only to expectations for staff workers in the upcoming discussions and examples we cite. As we lay out the complementary aspects of social practice—transformational design and motivational coaching—in the chapters that follow, we are fully aware that the application of these techniques can be extended beyond staff. We are also aware that we are speaking of a relatively embryonic field of professional practice that is in need of ongoing development. In presenting this information, we hope that it will be viewed as an exposition of our understanding to date that is open to reformulation and expansion. We present our understanding here as an invitation to others in the field of mental health, as well as to those in social and organizational development in general, for further reflection and innovation.

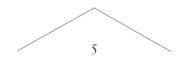

5

TRANSFORMATIONAL DESIGN

The medium is the message.

—MARSHALL MCLUHAN

By 1962, the original building housing Fountain House could no longer accommodate its increasing membership. The moment was ripe to build a new and larger house. John Beard supervised every aspect of the building's construction. He regularly reviewed the blueprints and contributed significantly to their specifications. Beard was eager to create the appearance of a non-institutional environment at Fountain House and wanted the membership to feel proud when attending it. Deinstitutionalizing the physical appearance of the building, however, was not enough. Beard's environmental design was also guided by an overriding sense of restorative purpose. Beard was always clear that it was not the concrete activities of the workday per se that were recuperative. As expressed in the response to the question raised by the interviewer in chapter 4, the social processes that these activities engendered, in which members and staff worked together, provided a means, a prosthetic, to support recovery. In the construction of the new building, therefore, Beard sought to include elements that would attract member interest and that fostered mutual respect and collaboration among members and staff. For example, he purposely designed the kitchen area for the new building without large areas for food storage. Instead of relying on deliveries by outsiders, members and staff would have to go out daily and buy whatever food was needed for the day's meals. In this way he transformed everyday activities such as food preparation into meaningful and shared tasks.

Throughout construction, Beard held to the conviction that the structures that organize Fountain House are expressive and that the social interactions of those who occupy its premises are molded by the dispositions cemented into its walls. As he once observed in a variation on McLuhan's aphorism, "Whatever you create . . . will communicate itself" (Propst, 1967). Thus Beard went about designing the new building with many facets that provided opportunities for members to contribute to the operation of the house in ordinary, worthwhile ways and that provided opportunities for interaction and personal exchange among members and staff.

Beard's attention to detail in this regard was legendary. Instead of being automated, the telephone switchboard was to be operated by members. Brass kick plates were affixed to the bottom of doors as a touch of refinement; the same brass plates provided a useful work opportunity, as they called for regular polishing. To keep the environment inviting, members and staff from the horticulture unit bought and displayed fresh flowers each week. Staff workers, to be effective in their role of engaging the membership, had to transform these social processes to be as inviting and reassuring as possible. This aspect of the staff role, called transformational design, is the subject of this chapter.

Our use of the term *transformational* here focuses on the attention given to the cultural (Schein, 1985) and structural predispositions of the environment that support individual motivation, empowerment, and change. As transformational designers, staff workers focus on how the activities of the house are framed (rather than on one-on-one interventions with members, which is the focus of motivational coaching, discussed in chapter 6). Transformational design makes activities accessible and relationally supportive by applying the fundamental principles of a working community—by (1) implementing a workday framework where activities are real and meaningful (and not simulated treatments); (2) infusing the need to be needed; (3) being respectful and evocative of member choice; and (4) fostering side-by-side relationships in planning and implementing the various tasks and activities.

In this respect, transformational design represents the expression of a *person-in-environment* perspective that is a characteristic of professional social work (Council on Social Work Education, 2008; Kemp, Whittaker, & Tracy, 1997; Kondrat, 2008). In a person-in-environment perspective, changing public expectations and societal structures is paramount. As widely practiced in the twentieth century by social workers who organized settlement houses for newly arriving immigrants to America, a person-in-environment approach assumed that the social and economic environment in which immigrants lived impeded their successful functioning. Settlement house social workers advocated on behalf of the individuals with whom they resided for the provision of needed public services or fought political or economic policies that undermined the potential of their lives. According to Sheafor and Horejsi (2006), "Concern over factors in both the immediate and distant environments is central to fulfilling social work's mission" (p. 9). This focus on the impact of social conditions on the individual continues to set social work apart from the other helping professions and is indicative of social practice at Fountain House.

In this chapter, we will explore how the practice of transformational design converts everyday social processes so that members are assured that they have a rightful place and no longer feel excluded. On the contrary, they can even make meaningful contributions. We will also consider what skills are required of staff in order to create welcoming and stimulating conditions that mitigate the social stigma associated with mental illness. In this regard, we will explore the major structural domains of the Fountain House working community that most directly concern transformational design: shared decision making, organizing the enterprise, and advocacy. We will address each of these social processes by defining its importance to the overall objective of supporting member recovery, and we will suggest techniques, such as consensus decision making or modeling, that Fountain House has found effective in contributing to successful member involvement. Whatever the task at hand, staff workers at Fountain House are expected to arrange the activity so that it is accessible to all and promotes involvement and success. Specifically, staff workers are expected to view their own involvement as collegial in nature and to call upon member talents, while respecting the members' choices about how they assume responsibility for the operation of the house. Thus, what Beard worked to achieve as a physical architect in the construction of the new building on West 47th Street, all staff are expected to replicate as social architects in their day-to-day dealings with members. Practically speaking, this means that all staff must practice the mandates of transformational design. Whether one is the executive director, a program staff worker providing direct services to members, or an ancillary staff worker, such as a secretary or accountant, he or she is expected to take the initiative and design the work space as an environment in which members are welcome to participate. Even in such traditional administrative and staff activities as new-member intake, the hiring, training and evaluation of staff, fund-raising, public relations, and evaluation of program effectiveness, members at Fountain House are to be found actively contributing their talents.

Consensus: Shared Leadership in Decision Making

Shared leadership in decision making is a powerful tool in transforming a social environment into a collaborative working community. At a minimum, it may only be a matter of making transparent the source and reasoning for a decision, particularly when unilateral decisions are made by the board of directors, the director, or an individual unit or staff person within the Fountain House community. More often, however, shared leadership in decision making is achieved by fostering consensus on common goals.

At Fountain House, consensus lays the foundation for building a working community that is respectful and evocative of member choice. It is also a particularly applicable technique because it encourages the value of collaboration that is indicative of our community. In effect, the practice of shared decision making through consensus builds a basis for collective achievement by seeking common agreement of participants to a proposition or specific course of action. It advances the inclusive participation of all stakeholders by pursuing compromises and broad agreement in achieving a collective course of action and dealing with minority objections without alienation. It avoids the divisiveness of voting that results in separating the group into winners and losers, or into the "us" versus "them" of autocratic leadership. In sum, shared decision making fosters the formation of a vital community in which members and staff can be observed working side by side in planning and contributing to the mission and goals of the organization.

Additionally, shared decision making results in solutions that better serve a community endeavor. Consensus is an effective group learning tool to pool ideas, generate insights, and analyze successes or failures related to initiative goals and outcomes. Kevin Bradley, an experienced clubhouse director, captures the opinion of many regarding decisions made through consensus: "The quality and thoughtfulness of the decision we reach as a community is superior to decisions I reach alone in my office" (Bradley, 1995).

At Fountain House, it is in the context of the daily morning and afternoon unit meetings that the principle of shared leadership becomes routinized. Rudy Giuliani, the famed mayor of New York City, was accustomed to speaking about the importance of his morning staff meeting in tackling the immediate needs of the day. Like Giuliani's morning meetings, unit meetings at Fountain House are akin to menu planning for the day's events. Unit meetings are where the day's duties get hashed out, deciding how particular projects will be readied and who is going to prepare what. Unit meetings can involve discussions in which the relevance of tasks is clarified and related to group goals, as well as to broader organizational goals. At these meetings, plans are also made to reach out to absent members, to expand access and utilization of unit services by the rest of the community, and to organize cooperation with other activity groups. In effect, Fountain House members participate in making decisions about the broader operation of the house within the context of these daily meetings. And, in this place where choice is so fundamental to member recovery, unit meetings provide members with the opportunity to determine their own personal contribution in these matters, which is essential to gaining a sense of empowerment within a recovery process. The daily meetings thus provide the framework for members to achieve their own sense of meaning and purpose in how they want to manage their recovery, and thus they can also achieve a sense of their own identity. As expressed by Deci (1995), "Choice is the key to self-determination and authenticity" (p. 10). This slice of life is played out over and over, every day, in the meetings of the various work groups at Fountain House.

Unit meetings are also a good example of the dynamics of "primary groups" (Cooley, 1909) and of how members become constituent partners in a group process. Typically, primary groups are small social groups (e.g., a family or social club) that are characterized by face-to-face association and cooperation, and whose enduring relationships are marked by shared activities and participants' concern for one another. Communications within such groups shift back and forth between the necessities of getting a job done and the building of relationships. Unit meetings foster such diverse exchanges. A sense of solidarity arises within the group by being needed to do the work, having the right to choose one's level of participation, and sharing in the decision-making process. Members are supported by the group to engage in experiences and to take risks. The meetings also provide for moments to recognize the work of those done on behalf of the community. Solidarity is further enhanced by the sharing of personal information. The meetings become platforms for announcements that promote the group's sense of connectedness with one another. During these meetings members and staff share stories that reveal personal interests or information that they'd like the group to know—a movie they like or perhaps an experience from the weekend past. As a result, unit meetings confer a feeling of belonging, the "we feeling" talked about by Cooley that results in a renewed sense of personal identity, relatedness, and accomplishment.

In adopting the practice of daily unit meetings, Fountain House capitalizes on the dynamic aspects of small social group communications. It is within the transactions of the unit meeting that the broad social welfare purposes of personal productivity and social inclusion are first realized in the individual lives of members. Thus a consensus approach broadly distributed throughout the operations of the house through daily unit meetings supports the development of individual growth in self-efficacy while contributing to improving the common good of the organization. And staff workers responsible for transformational design of the operation are expected to be proficient in running meetings and discussions. Staff skills must variously include listening, mindful consideration, empathy, inspirational motivation, and the ability to recognize a job well done. Approaches to issues that are basically collaborative in nature (in which guidance is directive without being manipulative or dictatorial) require staff workers to be accountable for the outcomes of their work without having control over the processes that engender them. It is exciting to watch skilled practitioners of shared decision making as they impart a palpable energy to an undertaking and generate a visible sense of shared ownership through cooperation. They demonstrate clarity in communications, skills in building agreement on objectives, and personal authenticity. Shared leadership also demonstrates how social justice can be achieved on the mundane level of an everyday meeting by ensuring that individuals with mental illness are not denied access to managing a fundamental activity of an organization—the discussion of its present and future goals—on the basis of a diagnosis or a certain level of functioning. Ultimately, it is this value for and practice of shared decision making, combined with an expectation of member responsibility, that demonstrates respect for members, and that empowers and facilitates their autonomous action and growth in recovery.

Organizing the Daily Enterprise

As a working community, Fountain House is organized around meeting individual member needs through the provision of community support services, such as housing, employment, and education. As Waters (1992), a longtime clubhouse practitioner, explained:

> The work that is performed by the members and staff of any clubhouse should be born, and naturally flow from, the needs of the membership of that clubhouse. Looking at it in even more

fundamental terms, the work of a clubhouse should be based on assisting people in meeting their basic human needs: needs such as being wanted and needed; needs that range from food and shelter, to acceptance and recognition, to employment and relationships. If we build our clubhouses around the central idea of developing environments in which people get their basic needs met, then the work we all do in our clubhouses to build these environments should be meaningful. (p. 43)

At the same time, attention is paid to those systems that sustain the daily operations of the organization, such as data collection, communications, and serving meals. In this way, the unit makeup of Fountain House mirrors the community's twofold needs. Some units are devoted to addressing the aspirations of members for education, health, or employment—needs that support the members in living successfully in society; other units attend to the operation of the house by preparing food (the culinary unit), arraying outcome statistics for reporting purposes (the research unit), and attending to communications (the clerical unit).

Each of these activity groups, or units, has a life of its own, and functions within a defined space in which staff and members collaborate. These activities take on the usual organizational scaffolding of any task by defining purpose, organizing work flow, analyzing failures, and celebrating success. On a daily basis staff perform a strategic function in the formation, operation, and eventual success within these various activity groups. Like the director on a movie set (who arranges the stage, confers with the actors on their lines, and announces coffee breaks), transformational design calls for the organization of the social structure of these groups by defining the purpose of their activities, breaking them down into their constituent parts, demonstrating how to perform individual tasks (i.e., modeling) so as to make them more manageable, and celebrating success. In this process transformational design at Fountain House reflects the four principal sources for the development of a sense of self-efficacy, which Bandura (1997) suggests is a critical factor in a person's ability to influence and determine the course of his or her own life.

The Working Community and Self-Efficacy

Albert Bandura is a major contemporary theorist in the field of cognitive psychology and the philosophy of action. He takes an agentic perspective that views the individual as self-organizing, proactive, and capable of affecting change in his own life conditions. The sense of self-efficacy, or how the person views his or her ability to influence the external environment, is central to his theory. Its functionality affects all aspects of a person's life, from influencing the formation of one's self-concept to shaping how one makes choices in the setting of goals, and how one faces challenges or interprets failures. "Efficacy beliefs," Bandura (1997) stated, "regulate aspirations, choice of behavioral courses, mobilization and maintenance of effort and affective reactions" (p. 4). Ultimately, psychologists like Bandura assert that increases in self-efficacy contribute to a person's ability to lead a more productive and happy life.

Bandura points to four stimuli that promote this sense of self-efficacy: actual experience, modeling, social persuasion, and individual physical and psychological factors. In the sections that follow, we describe how staff and others, in paying attention to these triggers when organizing the work of the day, can redefine the environment as an engaging and supportive place where members can take action and even consider assuming risks. Our discussion here focuses on strategies that spark member motivation to participate in house activities. Throughout, we will explore how the tasks and skills expected in transformational design can support members' eagerness to regain their place in a community once obstructed by their mental illness.

Deconstructing Work Processes

In structuring a working community to support member participation in making a contribution, we know that some members will come in daily, some part-time, and some only sporadically. It is therefore crucial that the structures of Fountain House complement member behavior and be accepting of members who come for only part of a day, or who come one day and not another. In no way can the arrangements of a working community appear to discredit those who do not attend on a regular basis or interpret the inconsistency in member attendance as any lack of commitment or resolve on their part. On the contrary, the organizational culture should recognize such decisions for the values they articulate—namely, that members are assuming responsibility for their own mental well-being and forging the reality of their own recovery. Staff must be supportive of member choice, and welcoming to them and their contributions when they do attend.

There are certain structural realities, therefore, that transformational design takes into account in organizing the work of groups when the members of the community are free to come and go as they decide best. Intermittent attendance requires that jobs be broken down into their constituent parts. Such a practice guarantees task continuity so that a member can step into the flow of an activity, even midstream, and easily pick up how to do it. This practice also demonstrates how deeply member choice is honored at Fountain House: no member is excluded because the job has already begun. Because of the possibility of irregular attendance, work units frequently have job description sheets readily available as visual aids for displaying the steps in completing an activity (Kaufman, 2002). Job sheets can be organized in binders for reference or may be posted on a wall in plain sight for everyone to read. Such forethought expands the accessibility of tasks beyond those who regularly attend, as Kaufman has noted: "When too many things are kept in the knowledge of too few, then work is not accessible and available to everyone" (p. 68). In contrast, units at Fountain House are imaginative in displaying work information so that it is widely accessible. Units typically feature open areas for planning, with a large board listing all the work assignments of the day followed by the names of those who are taking responsibility for individual tasks. They allocate separate spaces for various work areas. Task boards and file cabinets systematically organize topic areas. The units attractively display information on the status of members in the unit by shifting pictures of individual members among categories listed on the wall—"Working," "In School," "Outreach"—so that appropriate contact can be maintained. The units thus utilize visible space to advertise the work and be open to member choice.

Fountain House staff workers are expected to know how to break routine jobs down into their constituent parts and how to cogently display this information. The importance of such forethought and preparation cannot be overestimated. According to Bandura (1997), experience (a.k.a. enactive attainment) is the most important factor in determining a person's sense of self-efficacy; it provides "the most authentic evidence of whether one can muster whatever it takes to succeed" (p. 80). If a particular activity is broken into its constituent parts, members can learn the separate parts of the job and move from one stage of the process to the next when they are ready to advance. This experience of incremental successes breeds confidence in self-efficacy. Breaking tasks down into incremental steps allows for both access and incremental learning. It makes the possibility of achievement a reality for people whose previous failures have inhibited their motivation to act. Thus, deconstructing the work is one of the tools in the hands of staff for transforming a normal human activity into a socially supportive event.

At Fountain House, the potential for a multiplicity of performances is another key that opens the door for self-appraisals and experiences of incremental success. The public nature of all activities and meetings and the pervasiveness of participant interaction and freedom of movement at Fountain House create many diverse opportunities for enactive attainments to occur that are rarely replicated in mental health facilities. As Jackson (2001) has observed of people suffering from mental illness: "Psychologically isolated by illness that affects thoughts, feelings, and behaviors, they are, in addition, socially isolated from the everyday experiences of work and social connections. Individuals find few opportunities for positive self-appraisals as patients or clients in hospitals or institutions" (p. 63). In contrast, in a working community the willingness of members to contribute presents a wide range of opportunities for self-efficacy to develop.

Modeling

With member participation as the goal, consideration must be given to ensuring that those who do not know what to do in a particular situation have available to them the resources needed to become involved. In this respect ignorance and lack of requisite skills represent a structural barrier to participation, one that demands attention. Resourceful teachers must be always available to instruct in how a job, from the ordinary to the daunting, gets done whenever a lack of requisite skills causes members to hesitate or withdraw.

Access to instructional competence, then, is an important aspect of transformational design. Again according to Bandura (1997), "model competence is an especially influential factor when observers have a lot to learn and models have much they can teach them by instructive demonstration of skills and strategies" (p. 101). It is for this reason that Fountain House expects staff and others to be teachers, acting as inspirational role models, bolstering progressive successes in the work activity groups, and motivating members to achieve more than they thought possible.

Modeling (or vicarious experience from the member's point of view) involves demonstrating how to go about a particular task or how to handle a given social situation. At its most basic level, the teacher must know all of the instrumental information needed to complete a task if modeling is to succeed. Someone must be competent and ready to step in and show members, who may feel unsure about their ability to perform a job, just how doable the task actually is. They must be able to explain to others how a work process flows and indicate the performance levels required for successful completion. Members need to know the tools that they will employ, and staff and others should be ready to teach them how to use and care for those tools.

Conversely, failure to give this information may have a negative effect on the member's sense of solidarity with the group. An automatic disincentive is created when the aims are obscure and the performance objectives ambiguous, as it means the participants have no basis for determining how much effort to expend, how long to sustain it, and how to define or correct mistakes. Ill-defined tasks become unimportant and have no power to motivate engagement or challenge low self-esteem. Knowing the goals of the undertaking and their associative values and meanings motivates productive action on the part of the membership. Conversely, any vagueness or ambiguity about the meaning or importance of an activity communicates a general lack of concern or caring, which the member can easily translate as a lack of "concern for me." Eventually the member without proper direction may do nothing, or do parts of the task sporadically, or not even show up. This kind of outcome is a failure for the member and for the community.

Fountain House is fertile ground for modeling opportunities since, according to Bandura, the larger the size of the membership and the greater the volume of activities involved, the more pervasive the occasions for modeling.[1] One has only to review the whiteboards used to identify the work of each day to appreciate the breadth and diversity of the options open to members for involvement. Tasks written on the boards include giving a house tour, leading a unit meeting, taking photographs, doing a computer search, traveling to High Point to take part in administering shots to the alpacas, stalking cucumbers, answering the phone, interviewing people throughout the house and writing an article for the newspaper, organizing an advocacy effort, learning about hydroponics, repainting a room, replacing burnt-out lightbulbs, attending a block meeting, conducting a job search, developing a website, mastering Medicaid rules. The list is endless. Since the pursuits of Fountain House are anchored in diverse work roles and broad social interactions, there exists a breadth of opportunities for modeling that satisfies the persuasive power of numbers and multiplicity advocated by Bandura for modeling to be effective. Likewise, the likelihood that members will achieve the positive outcomes of renewed sense of self-worth and self–efficacy increases.

Bandura views the effectiveness of modeling in changing behavior as a by-product of a resulting comparative self-appraisal. There are many factors that determine one's judgment of similarity. People who are similar or slightly higher in perceived ability provide a powerful and relevant modeling opportunity. Age, sex, educational attainment, degree of overt pathology, hospitalizations, and so on are modeling influences, even though they are spurious indicators of performance success. Nevertheless, if a member observes the success of another member within the same work group—even if the two members have widely different characteristics—the potential for building self-efficacy and the motivation to participate increases.

For example, when a member at Fountain House sees another member performing an activity, the thought occurs: "If he or she can do it, then so can I." When members see other members accomplishing tasks, their self-efficacy and the likelihood that they may change their own behavior and take more risks increases, particularly if the member judges the individual to be similar to himself. As Bandura (1997) notes, "Seeing or visualizing people similar to oneself perform successfully typically raises efficacy beliefs in observers that they themselves possess the capabilities to master comparable activities" (p. 87).

More significantly here, the fact that members are role models for other members can be strategically utilized by staff to maximize a member's self-efficacy. Staff workers can adopt strategies that employ members as models. For example, when a member teaches another member, as an academic tutor or in a work activity, the fact that both collaborators are members can be sufficient to have a positive influence. Or, pairing a member who is competent in an activity, such as guiding tours, with a member who wants to learn that activity raises the possibility that the member will acquire the skills to do the task successfully. Vivian, a member who was particularly proud of her work as a teacher in the distance-learning college operated at Fountain House, put it this way in an e-mail message (August 18, 2012):

> I returned in 2001 after taking a disability retirement. I had a B.A. in Sociology and an M.S. in Library Science. It was very important to me to do something useful in retirement. The last ten years of my work history I had been a children's librarian. I didn't always get along with the other staff but the children loved me and I loved them in return. I ran all sorts of programs for them. After a few years as a member at Fountain House, I was asked to teach a satel-

lite college course in anthropology. I agreed and then a week before the course was to begin, I backed out. I assumed that would be the last time I had such an opportunity. But that is not the Fountain House way. After my self confidence returned, I was asked again. I considered it a great honor to teach.

My first class was four students. One was an older gentleman who had been a Fulbright scholar before becoming ill. The other three were young adults with some college who wanted to earn the three credits but also sharpen their study skills and return to college. I told the class I would study the material and present it to them but I wasn't an anthropologist so it should not come as a surprise if I didn't have an answer to their questions. I encouraged class discussions and tried to make it as much like a college class as I remembered. We took class trips to the Immigrant Museum, the Darwin Exhibit and Ellis Island. I noticed the students let me off the hook, so to speak and I did the same for them. We took a trip to the library to do research for term papers. It was a real college class without anxiety as far as I could arrange it. I had the pleasure of seeing one of my students get her B.A., two more return to college and two teach in the satellite college themselves. On the wall in my bedroom is a framed Certificate of Appreciation for my teaching.

Member modeling benefits not only the receiver of the information. The role of teacher enabled Vivian to retain her own self-esteem and feel worthwhile, despite her age, as she assessed the impact she had on the increased self-confidence and successes of her students. In effect, members of Fountain House are exposed to other members in a multitude of different settings—working in work activity groups during the day, socializing in the evening or during holiday programs, at special events, at transitional employment, and at numerous other planning or committee meetings. The pervasiveness of such opportunities for people suffering from mental illness holds important ramifications for the success of the working community and is one of the reasons for its greater potential for recovery in comparison to other mental health settings.

While pervasive modeling is part of the effectiveness of the Fountain House community, it has frequently been the source of widespread misunderstanding and misjudgments of what actually goes on there, particularly among professional educators in social work. When, for example, professors hear their graduate students who are interning at Fountain House describing their experiences of the day as "watering plants" or "operating the Hobart industrial dishwasher," they recoil. This is not what graduate students are being trained for. Unfortunately, in these cases, both the professors and their students are missing the significance of what occurs at Fountain House. They race to judgments based on appearances and overlook what lies beneath activities in which staff interns are exercising an essential strategy in fostering individual self-efficacy. As Bandura (1997) explained,

> Cognitive regulation of motivation and action requires performers to have some idea of what they are trying to attain and informative feedback about what they are doing. If they are not aiming for anything in particular or they cannot monitor their performance, they are at a loss to know what skills to enlist, how much effort to mobilize and how long to sustain it and when to make corrective adjustment in their strategy. (p. 66)

Interns and others at Fountain House assume modeling roles throughout the day to provide members with just the type of information they need so as not to lose interest. These roles have significant effects, for modeling even the simplest of tasks, we suggest, conveys formative consequences for members and their recovery.

The Utility of Perceived Relevance in Modeling

To be effective in transformational design, Fountain House staff need to be more than knowledgeable and skilled in accomplishing various work tasks. Defining the purpose of a task at Fountain House goes beyond the understanding of the instrumental nature of any activity. It is not enough to identify the purpose of an undertaking such as proofreading a newspaper so that people will understand what is written, or setting up a watering crew to go around the house so that the flowers will not wilt. Even under circumstances in which members may feel capable of doing the job, they may be left completely unmotivated when the job's social utility—the meaning for them personally—is absent. Defining utility, therefore, requires that the meaning of a task be extended from how and why it works to including its social utility. Staff must open the window to the motivational value inherent in Fountain House as an enterprise committed to recovery and social integration of its membership and how each member's involvement contributes to this end. A responsibility of every work group, therefore, is to establish its social goal or purpose by relating specific tasks to their demonstrable impact on individuals in the community at large. And since the accomplishment of any activity or service at Fountain House is dependent on its relevance to those who will perform the action, there must be an immediacy of perceived relevance in the minds of the contributors, the membership.

In the culture of Fountain House, in which neither financial incentives nor consumer demand for products or services is the driving incentive, meeting the visible needs of other members is what gives meaning to work and motivation to the membership. It is the immediacy of aiding someone who is standing right before you that provides meaning in the situation and the motivational hook. "Can you do this for me?" "Can you help her?" These are the common requests heard on the unit. Members are acutely aware of the results of their actions that benefit other members. When a member responds with eagerness, the awareness associated with his or her contribution is enhanced, and his or her self-worth and purpose are defined in relation to the community.

The leadership within a working community is entrusted with establishing "the immediacy of perceived relevance" of a task. The sheer size of Fountain House, however, makes this aspect of that responsibility particularly challenging. Given its multiple goals, the size of its membership, and its diverse array of working groups (units, resource areas, committees, and ad hoc projects), the principle of "immediacy of perceived relevance" presents a unique challenge within Fountain

House in motivating member participation. The tangible social purpose of an activity does not always lie within the immediate view of the primary group or unit that members work in. When an individual need resides in another unit or in an administrative resource group, an additional layer of appreciation is required to connect the needs of members and those satisfying their needs. For example, the educational unit advises not only its own members but also members in other units on applying for financial aid. More remotely, much of what the research unit does in terms of attendance data is justified by claims provided from external agencies for public funding. In each of these situations, recognition of the immediate need may not rely on any face-to-face contact within the unit, the primary group structure of the house. Transformational design demands that communication on the importance of work for the house or individuals in the house needs to be attended to. Although an activity may have little immediate perceived relevance, it does fulfill an important community function, which if adequately understood can be embraced by most members as relevant. In order to bring full intelligence and meaning to this process, therefore, the leadership of each unit is accustomed to educating its members as to the nature of its activities and how they satisfy the broader welfare of the whole house. This in turn becomes another motivational tool to nudge members to volunteer their assistance in a particular task.

Likewise, units and work groups must help others understand their purpose and the importance of their activities to the whole house by clearly advertising the nature and benefits of their services. In those instances when that service, unlike preparing meals or maintaining fresh flowers throughout the house, does not relate to an immediate human need, the group must engage in activities that educate and motivate members of the community in order to attract utilization of its services. One of the major ways that the meaning of a group's constituent activities gets defined is to make vigorous use of the many forums and communication media available at Fountain House. Daily and weekly news sheets tell everyone what is happening and discuss the issues of the day. Community meetings and regular task force or project meetings are held to discuss the many issues and significant events that relate to the group. In a community like Fountain House, however, where the need for communication goes beyond the instrumental and must include information demonstrative of the values underlying the organization in order to get the job done, there is a strong relationship between the level, degree, and type of expressive communications employed and their ultimate effectiveness. According to Etzioni (1961), the ultimate effectiveness in communities like Fountain House, which have strong constituent ideals, relies on the declaration of these values in channels of communication by its organizational representatives. At Fountain House, the nature and quality of the social climate must become an ingredient in the diet of routine communications.

Social Persuaders Celebrating Successes

The final stage of organizing work group activities is structuring them with opportunities for public acknowledgment of a task well done and for the recognition of the special contributions of individual members to the community. Beard understood that there are two factors in the equation for side-by-side collaboration. He needed a public platform so that the members would view an activity as personally possible (and so be won over to join in). He also needed a public platform for others, so that they, seeing what members were capable of, would respond with appreciation for those contributions. Beard once observed that although it was once thought that the advent of medications would eliminate mental illness, such aspirations were unrealistic. Beard understood the broader complexities of the illness in terms of the reluctance of societies to permit people with mental illness to participate in public activities. Pills alone were not going to break down the invisible walls of prejudice that prevented people with mental illness from regaining a normal life and returning to work. With Fountain House, Beard confronted the antipathy of society toward the presence of people living with mental illness in its midst by challenging expectations and transforming them from fear and prejudice into amazement and gratitude. A colleague attending training at Fountain House explained the wisdom of Beard's insight with a simple remark:

"Pills do not say 'thank you.'" Pills do not invite people with mental illness to assume roles as productive and cherished members of a community. As Bandura (1997) has confirmed, "The persuasory framing of influences that bear directly on self-efficacy appraisal are most evident in social evaluations of performance attainments" (p. 103). Recognizing member success illustrates well the importance that Bandura places on verbal persuasion as a means of strengthening people's belief that they possess the capabilities to achieve what they seek. Such information is conveyed for the most part in the evaluative feedback given to performers. As a result, even among those who harbor self-doubts, positive appraisals help to mobilize effort and lead people to try harder. Julius Lanoil, for example, recalled an incident from his past about Sally, a member of Fountain House, that illustrated the point well:

> I remember Sally, a member who assisted me in the thrift shop but who was fearful of waiting on customers. William was another member of the thrift shop group who enjoyed the retail selling aspect of thrift shop work. One afternoon, we became unusually busy and as luck would have it most of us were engaged away from the store making a large pickup of merchandise. I was later told that William was upset that Sally refused to help him with the customers but that she eventually relented as she saw the difficulty that William was having relating to the customers and packing their purchases and working the cash register. At our meeting the next day Sally was given a round of applause and then to my surprise and delight, volunteered to work on the sales floor as a regular work assignment. From then on, Sally, a usually quiet, reserved and fearful person, started to volunteer for everything. She covered placements when members were out and became active in planning our recreation programs. Soon she started her own job placement at Benton and Boles, an office placement requiring a lot of interaction with other employees.

For Sally, to attempt something slightly beyond her comfort level required not only an opportunity to perform the job but also openly expressed recognition of her contribution and appreciation from her community. Achievement deserves recognition, and recognition in turn motivates even greater involvement and more profound accomplishments.

How one frames such feedback, however, is critical. It must be positive but realistic in appraisal without making disingenuous comments. Beard would tell the story about a staff worker helping a member clean a window. The member puts cleanser on the window and wipes it off in the middle, leaving the cleanser residue around the sides. If the staff worker tells the member that he did a good job, such feedback, Beard would explain, only reinforces a low opinion of his abilities and hurts the relationship. The member sees through the thinly veiled, disingenuous evaluation. The worker acted on the mistaken notion that positive evaluations are always good and always raise self-efficacy. They are always good and do raise efficacy beliefs, but only within a framework of sensitive, realistic, and truthful feedback. Again, Bandura (1997) acutely observed that persuasion done by a significant person "can bolster self change if the positive appraisal is within realistic bounds" (p. 101).

While celebrating individual accomplishments motivates participation, in the hands of a transformational designer, such celebrations also ritualize an important cultural value. We know that culture is an important transmitter of organizational values, frequently more powerful than policies or standard operating procedures (Deal & Kennedy, 1982). Organizational rituals foster culture all the time. In a community culture like Fountain House, the celebration of achievement must be ritualized if the organization is going to thrive. People at Fountain House appreciate how hoopla is a strong part of its culture. Recognizing that the act of taking responsibility for a piece of the operation is a critical aspect of supporting member recovery, the weekly house meeting at Fountain House begins with an invitation for members who got a job that week to stand up and identify themselves for public recognition. Some clubhouses display photos of their members holding enlargements of their first paychecks. These public rituals represent imaginative and powerful ways to put the membership on notice that return to the workforce is a central goal of the clubhouse mission. In the same way, effective transformational leaders grasp what a powerful tool the management of these cultural processes is and pursue public expressions of achievement wherever they can be found.

Finally, inspirational stories of successfully overcoming obstacles told by competent member role models at group meetings or monthly employment dinners tend to be more meaningful than a discussion of the skills involved or an emphasis on the success. "Observers may benefit more from seeing models overcome their difficulties by tenacious effort," according to Bandura (1997), "than from observing only facile performances by adept models" (p. 99).

Similarly, utilization studies of unit services serve as an exceedingly important tool in situations that demand a justification that goes beyond the immediacy of face-to-face contact. Utilization studies document success in establishing the purpose of an activity within the broader Fountain House community. Regardless of apparent interest in a particular service or its perceived inherent value, program managers are routinely expected to justify their expenditures. Program evaluation skills, therefore, are an important tool to help staff and others assess how successfully component activities within the community are addressing house goals and member needs.

Promoting Wellness to Enhance Sense of Self-Efficacy

Bandura readily recognized that an individual's self-efficacy and capacity for performance are affected by any number of personal factors, including intelligence and good health. In recent years Fountain House has arrived at renewed insight into this relationship between sound health and psychiatric recovery. Unfortunately, it took the premature deaths of several members of the Fountain House community to prompt the realization that action was needed to promote wellness within the membership. In the same way that member education, finding a job, or living in decent housing is attended to, the integration of wellness at Fountain House now represents a whole new domain for exploration and innovation.

Clearly poor health can impede a member's chances of landing a job. We know from experience that an employer is not willing to sustain the employment of a member who is constantly missing work because of sickness or taking time off for doctors' appointments. Results from a literature review on the health conditions of people with mental illness raise the issue into more stark relief. The most disturbing finding of all, however, is that the life expectancy for people with serious mental illness is twenty-five years less than that of the general population (Parks et al., 2006). The same report indicated that adults with serious mental illness have a higher incidence of disease, diabetes, and high blood pressure. Also, people suffering from mental illness receive on average inadequate or poor health care. Likewise, research on the connection between exercise and health found that the lack of sufficient physical activity was linked to seventeen unhealthy conditions, most of which are chronic diseases or risk factors for chronic diseases (Booth et al., 2000). The lack of sufficient physical activity, in concert with smoking, poor nutrition, and the weight gain that can result from second-generation antipsychotic medication have led to substantial health risks for adults with serious mental illness.

In a promising turn, these same studies indicate that embracing a healthier lifestyle can have positive effects. Both diet modification and exercise have been found to mitigate both diabetes and heart disease. And, as a result of many convincing studies, the surgeon general concluded in his report on physical activity and health that regular physical activity reduces the risk of dying prematurely in general and from heart disease in particular (www.cdc.gov/nccdph/sgr.htn). It also reduces the risk of developing diabetes, high blood pressure, and colon cancer, while reducing feelings of depression and anxiety. In other words, promoting physical well-being has considerable import for those suffering from mental illness.

With this information in hand, the whole Fountain House community was mobilized to find a resolution. A proposal was brought to the house for the formation of several working committees representing all the major constituents (members and staff, as well as board representatives and outside experts) of the Fountain House community; these committees would report back with specific recommendations for changes. A professional management consultant volunteered to guide the decision-making process. The subcommittees gathered information, consulted experts, and evaluated potential options. Consideration was given to both what to do and how it might be accomplished in the collaborative, strengths-based culture that is central to the Fountain House working community. Several major donors emerged to support an initial investment in hiring personnel and renovating the existing building. Ultimately, after two years of internal debate, the Fountain House response was to replace what had traditionally operated as a snack bar with a wellness unit. The wellness unit was given the mandate to integrate wellness awareness and practices throughout the house in terms of diet, physical activities, and access to quality medical, dental, and psychiatric care.

There is much that can be learned about the importance of transformative design in social practice from this response of Fountain House to address the concerns for member health. Fountain House was mindful and took its direction from the needs of the membership. It recognized that poor health among the membership was as much of a barrier to their mental health recovery as unemployment or school failure. We used research (social persuasion) to understand the urgency of the situation as well as to suggest possible avenues for development, and this information became a mandate to create new structures where none had previously existed. Fountain House followed a collaborative process (shared leadership in decision making) that granted input to all the principal stakeholders—members, staff, board members, experts, volunteers, donors—so that a broad consensus was developed for the final course of action, the formation of a new unit. It is the consistent application of these same values—mindfulness, research, innovation, and shared decision making—over time that accounts for the success of Fountain House in remaining a vital force in mental health practice.

The community employed the reality of the moment to explore opportunities for personal learning and development. In such circumstances, attention to the application of Bandura's influences is particularly apt. The daily workday presents myriad opportunities for real experiences (enactive learning), modeling, social persuasion, and support for maintaining good personal health. Staff workers and others must become skilled in structuring these opportunities properly so that access to all is ensured and social persuaders are readily available to provide encouragement and to structure public recognition of member accomplishments.

Community Support as Advocacy

Ultimately, transformational design extends beyond its location on West 47th Street and moves into the broader community to help members secure jobs, education, entitlements, housing, quality medical treatment, psychological and pharmacological assistance, and whatever else will facilitate a better quality of life for them. While the goal is the same—eliminating barriers to participation in the environment in which the members live—the role and the requisite skills are different. Outside the house, staff workers shift their approach from empowerment to advocacy. They need to enlist allies in speaking out against the prejudices of society and addressing government policies and regulations that undermine member efforts to become productive citizens in their communities. Fountain House has established its reputation over the years for speaking out against the prejudices of a society that denies people who are afflicted with mental illness their rightful place in jobs or housing. Its most famous effort in this regard was the development of transitional employment. More recently, in the 1990s, Fountain House was among the lead agencies in New York City that successfully advocated for reduced transit fares on public transportation for its members, along with all people with disabilities. In 2004, when the Bush administration introduced restrictions on access to public funding for post-secondary education—in effect denying to Fountain House members, as well as anyone with a mental illness, the only source of public funds to attend college—Fountain House members and staff challenged the legality of the regulations. Ultimately, Fountain House secured an exemption from the new regulations for anyone in the nation who suffers from a mental illness. Currently, Fountain House is a founding member of the

"Bring Change 2 Mind" national media campaign in the United States to eliminate the nation's tendency to stigmatize people suffering from mental illness.

Advocacy, then, is central to the function of transformational design. Advocacy expands the repertoire of staff and members alike and turns individual community support efforts (helping with entitlements, finding a job, schooling, or housing) into ways for people suffering from mental illness to live within society at large with personal respect and dignity. When staff workers of Fountain House advocate on behalf of members, they do so as an expression of social justice for a group that has been marginalized by society on the basis of their diagnosis. Advocates secure the rights of Fountain House members; the right to work and to go to school and the basic rights that come with citizenship in a democratic society, such as the right to information and the right to have a voice in decision making, are all part of concerns of the Fountain House community. In this respect, Fountain House staff workers promote social justice in the tradition that was established by workers in the settlement house movement: civil advocacy is the hallmark of the social work profession.

In summary, the practice of transformational design at Fountain House is to make work exciting and meaningful while removing any structural barriers to members' contributing their efforts. It is a complex job that expects staff workers to temper their natural instincts to get the job done with the selflessness of a generalist who recognizes talent in others rather than asserting their own expertise. Staff at Fountain House must be proficient in analytic and communication skills and possess a facility for group dynamics. Collaborative leadership, engaging members in modeling, and inspiring purpose are all standard tools in the hands of those who practice transformational design. Fountain House further expects its staff to be effective community-change agents in advocating for social justice for members. As public advocates, staff must have the ability to form alliances with other support agencies or institutions. In this way, the structures of Fountain House create an environment that empowers people who live in the isolation that is endemic to their illness to be freed from stigma, to regain a sense of belonging, self-efficacy, and accomplishment, and to become valued community contributors. Creating an accessible, stigma-free social structure alone, however, is insufficient to achieve this outcome. For its members to succeed in social reintegration, Fountain House also demands of its staff workers the skills of a trusted personal coach, as described in chapter 6.

6

MOTIVATIONAL COACHING

It is easier to sustain a sense of efficacy when there
are difficulties, if a significant other expresses
faith in one's capabilities.

—ALBERT BANDURA

Mark Glickman is a former member of Fountain House who now lives and works successfully in Southern California with his wife. His credits include a book, *Fountain House: Portraits of Lives Reclaimed from Mental Illness* (Flannery & Glickman, 1996), a documentary film on Fountain House, and a seat on the board of the International Center for Clubhouse Development. His life was not always this way. Glickman (2005) related that when he was twenty-four years old his father accompanied him to the front steps of Fountain House in New York City following his hospitalization for a mental breakdown. After an initial successful transitional employment, he was eager to return to college. He admitted, however, that he moved too quickly, failed miserably in his first semester of school, and dropped out of Fountain House for several years. Glickman refers to this period as his "lost years," due to the shame and disappointment he felt from failure. He subsequently returned to Fountain House and was able this time to transform his situation and move on with his life. Such sporadic initial involvement is not uncommon among our members.

Glickman's story is not unlike the stories of many others who are afflicted with severe mental illness. We know that mental illness is not just a disease that trips people up and causes them to lose their bearings as their young lives begin to unfold. The illness has pernicious consequences on the psychological state, social and economic status, and continuing quality of life of those who are affected. Members of Fountain House regularly experience symptoms of confusion, loneliness, social rejection, educational and employment failure, and loss of self-esteem. It is with this awareness of the pervasive impact of the illness on the personal functioning of its members that Fountain House has its staff workers build significant relationships with members.

Every member of Fountain House is expected to select a staff social worker to be his or her guide or mentor. Members can choose whomever they want, but they must choose. Likewise, staff are expected to assume a mindful responsibility for the progress of the members to whom they are assigned. John Beard inculcated this practice at Fountain House. When asked to describe Beard's approach, Bob Harvey, an early staff person there, recounted that Beard called him into his office one day and asked to see his member cards. Staff workers were expected to maintain information about the ongoing progress of each of their members on three-by-five cards. Beard recognized that a community designed to support individuals in psychiatric recovery required intervention on an individual basis. Thus he expected staff to form personal relationships with individual members as a crucial part of social practice at Fountain House. Fountain House continues this practice today in the form of motivational coaching.

Motivational coaching is the aspect of social practice that deals with the individual. In contrast to restructuring the social environment, which remains the focus of transformational design, staff workers as motivational coaches are expected to form one-on-one relationships with members to assist them in their recovery. Whereas transformational design addresses the results of prejudice structurally, motivational coaching pays attention to its impact on the individual. In this respect, the job of the motivational coach calls for reaching out to members in isolation, fostering a significant relationship with them to help bridge issues such as risk taking or anxiety, and assisting them in taking advantage of the opportunities that Fountain House or a broader society has to offer (such as employment, education, and housing). The job is varied and complex. It demands a flexible spirit and a professional disposition in dealing with the issues and problems that arise in one-on-one relationships.

Motivation characterizes the overriding purposeful nature of the one-on-one coaching relationship. These relationships among staff and members are instrumental in nature. They should not be judged in terms of the degree of affinity they generate but in terms of the members' success in finding a way to become involved and contribute in the settings in which they reside. Throughout, the posture is proactive, without being controlling, and strengths-based. This chapter will discuss the nature of motivational coaching, how it is established and fostered, and why it is central to producing the positive outcomes for members of regaining self-worth, purpose, confidence, and direction. Related issues that naturally arise from forming close human relationships with members—such as dealing with psychoses or dependency, or defining boundaries in terms of a social worker's professional codes of ethics—and its limitations are discussed separately in chapter 7.

Why One-on-One?

Why was Beard so adamant about the formation of one-on-one relationships? Why did he introduce the structural imperative of fostering significant staff–member relationships?

Fountain House as a working community is unique in that it purposely understaffs its operations. Most organizations hire sufficient staff and then hold them responsible for the completion of those tasks to which they are assigned. A working community like Fountain House, on the other hand, applies the principle of the need to be needed so that the jobs that need to be done are too numerous for the staff on hand to complete. In an organization in which staff workers are too few and the tendency for isolation is an inherent trait of a membership that suffers from mental illness, there exists the possibility that a particular member may be overlooked and fall through the cracks. Under such circumstances, the expectation of staff to form significant one-on-one relationships with members might strike one as a shrewd management technique, much like taking out an insurance policy against such a breakdown in services.

But Beard viewed fostering significant relationships with members as more than just a prudent management technique. He understood from his days spent on a back ward of Eloise, where his patients were overwhelmed by past failures and self-doubt, that individual interventions were necessary for participation in activity groups to take hold. Reaching deeply withdrawn individuals was a talent, as we have already noted, that Beard practiced with uncanny skill. Similarly today, staff workers at Fountain House find that building a trustful relationship with members opens up opportunities for staff to be helpful in situations that provoke anxiety or embarrassment in members. Having a significant relationship with a member means that the member is more likely to listen to advice on goal planning or learning survival skills. Modern studies have come to confirm Beard's insight in this matter. Anthony (2000), in devising a framework for a recovery-oriented system, states: "A common denominator of recovery is the presence of people who believe in and stand by the person in need of recovery. Seemingly universal in the recovery concept is the notion that critical to one's recovery is a person or persons in whom one can trust to 'be there' in times of need" (p. 160). Harding has also shared with us that having a "circle of friends" was a common element in the recovery cycle that she observed in her long-term studies of people suffering from serious mental illness living in Maine and Vermont (DeSisto et al., 1995a, 1995b). As illustrated in the transformational design discussion of chapter 5, there are many aspects of social practice at Fountain House that create an emotional congruity with members and facilitate their motivation to participate and their consideration as to the level of that participation. To these must be added a significant relationship with a staff worker. The complementary roles of transformational design and motivational coaching in social practice together create the positive practice results that ultimately define the community's effectiveness in supporting the recovery and social integration of the membership.

Our emphasis on the formation of one-on-one relationships has its roots in the nature of mental illness itself. The reality that is so troubling to people with severe mental illness—aside from the overt symptoms that define it—is the attitudes or behaviors that develop in the patient under treatment, like passivity or avoidance, that further exacerbate their condition. Such behaviors are the result variously of the impact of the illness, multiple hospitalizations, and the public stigma and rejection that accompany it. Additionally, these behaviors are not usually amenable to pharmacological interventions (Kirkpatrick et al., 2006). Therefore a major reason for our emphasis on the development of influential relationships between members and staff arises from the difficulty that members experience in overcoming these conditions. Helping members to come to terms with the negative symptoms of their illness[1] is achieved at Fountain House through the social practice of motivational coaching that reaches out to members to arrest their isolation, that supports their taking risks, and that seeks to dispel any anxieties that may arise from participation in a working community.

Why Coaching?

Coaching is a strengths-based technique consistent with current best practices in social work (Rapp & Goscha, 2006). In a coaching relationship, the goal is to maximize the aspirations and potential of the client by building on his or her strengths and skills. According to Kauffman and Scoular (2004), "The newest wave of coaching is based on the strength-building perspective of positive psychology, a perspective which is simple yet powerful in its assertion that a focus on strengths and values is a more effective way to increase performance and satisfaction" (p. 289). Coaching is not manipulative or coercive. In coaching, for example, staff workers do not make deals with members in order to win their cooperation, nor are there any agreements in which the resources of the house are made contingent upon participation or compliant behavior. Coaching is about empowerment—not about telling someone what to do or what not to do.

It focuses on helping individuals to determine for themselves what their own goals and aspirations are. As such, coaching is the concrete framework for staff who are working as colleagues "side by side" with members on the business of the house, where the client becomes "a co-active, equal partner" (p. 288). Such a posture assures a tight fit with the fundamental principle of a working community—namely, the members' right to choose the ways in which they will participate in the day's activities and the staff with whom they will work.

The concept of coaching is also what differentiates Fountain House from traditional talk therapy. The idea of coaching, which as described by Seligman (2003) is a part of positive psychology, is to maximize the potential of the client by building on his or her strengths and skills. Thus, while coaching involves processes that have the same goals as therapy in terms of helping people facilitate self-actualization, coaching is not therapy. Coaching achieves its goal through different means. As Kauffman and Scoular explain, "In therapy you look for the underlying source of the problem and help the client fix it. In coaching, you look for the strengths and help the client enhance them" (p. 290). At Fountain House we do not do traditional talk therapy. Rather, coaching is consistent with the processes in which staff relate to members in one-on-one problem solving and seek to influence their actions. It more aptly describes the uniqueness of our strength-based and non-medical approach to practice, the goal of which is to maximize the potential of the client by building on his or her interests and skills.

In effect, staff workers as motivational coaches face a daunting challenge, since member participation in the house is at once voluntary and essential for recovery. How staff workers navigate the personal divide of their job to motivate member engagement within a culture in which members' free choice is pervasive is the craft of the motivational coach. In the discussion that follows we will demonstrate how coaches take the initiative and reach out to members in isolation. We will describe how significant relationships build a personal sense of hope and trust among members that ultimately enables staff to help members move on with their lives.

Reachout

The major task of the motivational coach is to reach out to members who are absent or withdrawn. The act of reachout, or taking the initiative to extend one's hand in an offer of aid, acknowledges the isolation that members endure either as a result of their illness or as the consequence of the rejection they feel from a society that fears their presence. Members may be afraid to leave their home, they may appear to be trapped in psychotic symptomatology, or they may exhibit a flat affect and show no emotion at all. It is the responsibility of the motivational coach to take the initiative and reach out to members in isolation with an inviting hand.

From its beginnings, Fountain House viewed the act of reachout as an identifying characteristic of its methodology, differentiating it from the practice of other mental health facilities of the day. A board member in the 1950s described Fountain House's more proactive approach to social work:

> Formally much of social work practice was based on the old aphorism that although you could lead a horse to water, you could not make him drink. It was considered the function of an agency to prepare its special services, and on occasion even to advertise their availability, but, until recently . . . a social work agency did not drum up trade or entice a reluctant customer into its shop. The service was on the table, so to speak, and if the customer was hungry—physically, psychically, morally or emotionally—he could attempt to satisfy his needs with the aid of the resident personnel. It would lengthen this report unduly to detail all the ways in which a more dynamic, or if you will, more benignly acquisitive attitude is taken toward the members at Fountain House. (Wolf, 1958)

Thus, however one first encounters the individual, it is the responsibility of the motivational coach to initiate the conversation and to find some way to develop a meaningful, one-on-one relationship with that member.

Beard was famous for his ingenious ability to initiate an ordinary dialogue with his patients—he put candy under their pillows at night or wrote their names on the ceiling and asked them to identify their own names. John Delman, an early member of Fountain House who subsequently became an employee, tells the story. He worked closely with Beard and recalled accompanying him on a visit to the home of a member. Beard and the member got to talking about Boston and started to trade stories. Once a rapport was established, Beard moved on in the conversation and invited the member to return to Fountain House. The story describes how Beard looked for a point of entry with the member, a place of common interest and normalcy untouched by overt psychosis, that could form the basis for establishing a relationship. And once that link was forged, he had a way to re-engage the member in the fellowship of Fountain House.

Reachout is an existential component of the role of motivational coach and an enduring characteristic of the staff–member relationship. Staff workers must be impervious to rejection by members no matter how mature and friendly their relationship has become. They cannot take rejection personally, as mental illness has a chronic aspect that can surface at any moment. Rather, as in the following story about Steven, coaches must remain ever alert to any sudden changes in member behavior.

Steven, a young adult, was in and out of the hospital after he started college at New York University. After each hospitalization, he would return to school, become ill again, be hospitalized, and then return to school. On the advice of his psychiatrist he came to Fountain House and indicated upon intake that he was eager to go to work. Julius Lanoil, in his notes about his experiences at Fountain House, recalls:

> At that time, we were looking for members to work at Chock Full O' Nuts, a sandwich, soup, and coffee restaurant, which was a new group placement. The owner had given Fountain House complete operating responsibility. Steve had been at Fountain House for just one week but was very interested in trying the placement. I became Steve's worker and brought him to the placement to be trained. He

was a natural, learned the work quickly, and appeared happy being there. After two weeks of good work, however, he stopped coming. When I called his home I spoke to his mother, who informed me that Steve would be starting at New York University again. At a meeting that I set up with her and Steve, she argued for the importance of his continued education. I responded, with Steve's consent and the support of his psychiatrist, that he could benefit from staying at Fountain House, continuing on the placement, and helping in the Fountain House tutoring program. I suggested that in the seven months until the start of the next semester, the positive work experience and the supportive relationships at Fountain House would help Steve in his next try as a full-time student. Steve continued at Fountain House, completed the placement, and went on to another placement at Benton & Bowles, after which he returned to college. During the next two years Steve received a degree from NYU while maintaining a part-time job on weekends and continuing his tutoring at Fountain House and his relationship with me.

It is natural at times for members to drift or get distracted. Fortunately, the staff person in this case was alert and initiated immediate reachout when he noted a change in behavior. He was able to resolve the situation by emphasizing the importance of both school and work. Here the progress achieved at Fountain House was not lost; instead it was easily integrated with the member's new stage of development in returning to school. Given Steve's previous history of educational failure, his success is indicative of the effectiveness of the Fountain House approach that we subscribe to here.[2] The significant relationships that form between staff and members at Fountain House encourage members to remain involved and culminate in their recovery and regaining an outside life.

Furthermore, when members observe how interventions are successful with others, they are subsequently motivated to participate themselves. Some members find it hard to believe that their presence in the Fountain House community is truly valued by others because of their past failures or negative experiences. Yet when they see a staff person successfully reach out to a member who has become withdrawn, they begin to appreciate how the contribution of each individual is valued at Fountain House and begin to open up. Finally, early reachout can ferret out nonverbalized impediments to attendance and participation, and create among members a strong, genuine appreciation and a sense of being accepted, wanted, and needed.

Establishing Significant Relationships

Once contact has been established, each staff worker is expected to form a significant bond with the member. We have chosen the word "significant" to describe our practice because it implies both intensity and influential capacity—without disregarding member choice, which is indispensable in our craft. In our definition, a significant relationship is one that holds an influential capacity of one person over another. It expands the practice of coaching to encompass the likelihood that the feedback that the coach gives to members will be heard and evaluated without creating a feeling of being obligated or forced to act. It is akin to the experience of having a significant teacher. We all have had teachers, but a very few of us, if we have been lucky, have had teachers in whom there existed respect and trust that have had such a powerful impact on us that our lives have been changed by it. We describe these highly influential relationships as significant.

Additionally, a significant relationship minimizes the likelihood that a member may fall through the cracks. As practitioners, we know that the process of change is rarely a smooth progression of successful events. More often than not, it is a series of steps forward punctuated by some setbacks. When motivational coaches have developed meaningful relationships with members, members are much more motivated to stay the course. Staying actively involved with a member who attends sporadically also mitigates against an "out of sight/out of mind" attitude. It creates a sense of commitment among staff workers to do everything possible to keep their members' quality of engagement vigorous. This commitment does not always guarantee success, but it does increase the likelihood that the staff coach will be mindful if rehospitalization, reduced participation, or a plateau in the level of progress occurs.

Some may argue that a significant relationship between the motivational coach and a member, though it is one motivational tool, is not necessary for member success. While we recognize that some members move on with their lives without ever having a significant relationship with a staff worker at Fountain House, nonetheless, when a significant relationship exists, all feedback becomes more relevant and the staff coach is in a stronger position to have a constructive impact on a member's motivation and personal decisions. The trust that results from a significant relationship prepares members to hear the advice of another person when matters become troublesome, such as poor money management or unrealistic expectations. In other words, the effectiveness of the Fountain House working community is greatly enhanced when a significant relationship exists between a staff worker functioning as a motivational coach and a member. Forming a genuine relationship is a crucial aspect of meeting the goals and life aspirations of the members.

The value that members place on the Fountain House culture that considers personal relationships as a contributing factor in their success is evident from member responses to the question "What do you look for in staff?" Typically, responses to this question range from a sense of basic acceptance—that the staff person likes them or believes in them, or "she seems happy to hear from me"—to declarations of specific qualities. Good staff are "good listeners." "He cares." "She gave me a new idea." "She inspires me." "They help solve my problems" "He has a great sense of humor." Members do not even seem to mind being pushed, as they recognize the motivation behind the intrusion: "He gets me angry, but he's got heart." The result of such a special relationship is the acknowledgment of how comforting it is when a member states, "I can be myself and say anything to the staff." Our personal observations and discussions over the years with members and staff have convinced us that such relationships enhance feedback, facilitate a feeling of support, influence risk taking, and inspire staff and members to persevere. We consider the formation of significant staff–member relationships to be an essential component in mental health practice.

Forging a Significant Relationship

At the beginning of the relationship, staff workers must find the motivation within themselves to work with a new member and discover the incentives they will employ to invite that person to participate. Often a coach will find something about the member to like, appreciate, or respect. Beard was accustomed to saying that staff workers must find something healthy about the person to connect with—"even their hair or fingernails must be healthy." Though the imagery of this example is overstated, it underscores the strengths-based approach that distinguishes significant relationships at Fountain House. Staff workers bypass the focus of illness or deficit common in mental health assessments and draw on the aspects of the person that are of common interest to make critical interventions. Seligman has underlined this contrast in treatments with many of today's mental health professionals. He suggests that "people in the mental health professions have been more heavily interested in intricate theories of failure than on theories of success. When mental health professionals do their best work, they amplify strengths rather than repair weaknesses of their clients" (Seligman & Csikszentmihalyi, 2000, p. 7). Julius Lanoil relates the story of an early Fountain House member, William, who illustrated this point well.

William came to Fountain House in 1972. He hallucinated a lot, but had an ability to remember dates for all kinds of events in the past. He could also tell you on which day of the week a particular date would fall. This unique ability caught the attention of his staff worker. As Lanoil recalls,

> William had been hospitalized numerous times and had a confusing thought process which, in addition to the uninterrupted pattern

of hallucinations, made his initial impression difficult to tolerate. His staff worker however had a strong belief in his abilities and saw William as a challenge to his skill. His approach was to focus on William's strengths and pay little attention to his hallucinations or flighty thoughts. As William began working in the kitchen, his punctuality and helpfulness became important to his staff worker's efforts there and, irrespective of the symptomatology that William exhibited, the staff worker began to appreciate and respect William as a person of substance. Basic acceptance (which is the first element in the formation of a relationship) that the staff person offered William was eventually rewarded as he received much-needed assistance from William in the unit.

In this anecdote, the relationship between the staff worker and the member started with the staff person finding William's facility with dates to be remarkable. In other cases, interest might come from personality traits such as friendliness or a positive attitude. Some staff workers, as also illustrated in the above story, are drawn to new members because they present a great deal of overt pathology and represent a professional challenge. Whatever the initial appeal may be, its importance here lies in a staff person's getting to know a member from a perspective that sidesteps the illness, which in turn is met with a willingness to plunge into the work of the house.

Relationships Remove Barriers

There are many structural practices that make a supportive community like Fountain House appeal to members and call for their involvement, among them the practice of open communications and non-segregated space, the pervasiveness of opportunities where members' contributions are needed, or the public acknowledgments of member successes. These practices of the working community certainly lay the groundwork for facilitating member participation. But nothing can replace the power of a coach's removal of an obstacle that the member faces to make a member feel grateful and willing to reciprocate.

Motivational coaches are expected to ameliorate personal difficulties that stand in the way of member recovery. This is particularly important in the initial months of a member's association with Fountain House, during which any number of issues can become impediments to attendance.

When members first come to Fountain House, many arrive with unmet needs in various domains of life. At times they find it difficult to participate because of these circumstances. Sometimes these difficulties are verbalized; sometimes they are not. Members may be stressed because they do not receive adequate emotional support from other important relationships such as a treating psychiatrist, a family member, or an after-care agency worker. Other issues can arise, such as problems with finances, transportation, medication, food purchases, or negotiating benefits with the Social Security Administration. Finding immediate work and housing soon after hospitalization discharge is also a major concern of many new members. At times, a new member might feel intimidated by the size or energy level at Fountain House or be put off by bizarre behavior exhibited by an individual member. In any event, the resolution or removal of these initial impediments to participation not only makes it possible for new members to attend, but increases the prospect of their involvement. Additionally, it enhances the potential for influence in the staff-member relationship.

Peckoff, a member of Fountain House, has noted that it was the mindful intervention by a staff person that helped her resolve one of those unmet needs, a pending financial problem, that precipitated her involvement in Fountain House. Although she was initially reluctant, she eventually broke out of her isolation and began participating in the house, by becoming a tour guide. She explained:

> During this time, I was always looking around and noticed members and staff working on the switchboard, the newspaper, research projects and attendance. Members and staff would try to encourage me to get involved, and, though I did not at the time, something was going on because I came in mostly every day even though it took me an hour and a half to get there. One day, one of the staff

members came over to me and asked me if I would like to go to a tour guide meeting. That was the last thing I wanted to do. But because she had helped me to get financial assistance when I needed it, I said okay. That was almost 14 years ago, and I'm still a tour guide. (Peckoff, 1992)

Despite her initial reluctance to get involved, the urging of a staff worker who had previously helped her was a contributing factor to her coming out of herself. The experience became a major milestone in describing her journey from patienthood to personhood.

A somewhat more subtle element in relationship building involves the way in which a helping act is accomplished and perceived by the member. When members observe staff dealing with government bureaucracy, psychiatrists, family, and landlords on their behalf, they are impressed and grateful. But, when they become aware that a staff worker handles their issues with all their complex details with tenacity and care that guarantee success, they begin to see their staff worker as a special person. One member reflected that his staff worker "was dealing with the welfare people like it was for himself." John Beard referred to this practice as "completing the helping act," and Lanoil illustrates the point with an anecdote originally related by Beard: "A person in a vehicle stops you for directions. You tell him to go two blocks, turn right, then go to the third light and make a right, then at 46th Street, go left, etc. These directions are helpful but it would be better to write them down for the person. And can you imagine, Beard would conclude, the impact on the driver if you personally took him to his destination?"

Beard was adamant that staff workers take a generalist approach and see the implications of a member's declaration of need through to their natural conclusion. He considered it an effective technique in forming significant relationships with members while helping them overcome the impediments they faced. Practices at Fountain House, while seemingly the same as those of mental health case managers, differ in that they involve establishing these relationships while following through on all the various aspects of the services their clients are requesting. In this respect, case management at Fountain House has both an instrumental and a relational aspect. As illustrated in the story above, staff workers are aware that while they satisfy a member's immediate need they are also building an ongoing and supportive relationship for the long term.

In conclusion, successful reaching out to a new member, finding things about that member to like and/or respect, removing obstacles to his participation, and completing the helping act are initial practice elements of motivational coaches and the beginning of the establishment of a significant relationship.

Support for Risk Taking

When a person participates in activities that outstrip what they think they can reasonably accomplish—what Vygotsky describes in child's play as standing "a head taller than himself" (Vygotsky, 1978, p. 102)—personal growth is quickened. The experience of the successful completion of a formidable activity results in a clear change in self-evaluation. It can also have a profoundly positive effect on a member's future risk-taking efforts. As Bandura (1997) found, "Powerful mastery experiences that provide striking testimony to one's capacity to effect personal changes can also produce a *transformational restructuring of efficacy beliefs* that is manifested across diverse realms of functioning" (p. 53). Fountain House social practice similarly asserts that personal growth is the result of increases in self-confidence that occur when a person successfully completes a house activity and experiences mastery. Motivational coaches are in a unique position in such situations to foster participation and growth.

Some would contend that only similarly disabled persons can step in at this point to assist the members with their mastery of a situation. They would argue that only those who share the disability possess sufficient empathy to be of assistance (Borkman, 1999; Chamberlin, 1977, 1987, 1995). We contend, however, that everyone in the Fountain House community, irrespective of a disabling condition, can effectively support the member in developing a sense of self-efficacy. And while other modeling influences exist in the Fountain House community (such as the pervasive progress of other members), motivational coaches play an important role in engaging members to take a risk and "stand a head taller." Once a staff worker has gained the trust of members and is seen as knowledgeable, credible, and important to them personally, his or her support will have a great effect on them. As Bandura (1997) found, "It is easier to sustain a sense of efficacy when there are difficulties, if a significant other expresses faith in one's capabilities" (p. 101). Trust imbues staff workers with the prerequisite sense of credibility that permits their input to be heard without any diminution in the members' sense of self-actualization. Moreover, without these strong supportive relationships, members may progress only within their comfort zone, which would set a self-limiting plateau well short of their full potential, avoiding risk taking altogether. In effect, proactive, motivational coaches are important aids to the growth and self-actualization of the member, as the following anecdote demonstrates.

Lanoil remembers how John, a staff worker at the Club (an early replication of Fountain House in New Jersey) attempted to assist a member, Louis, who was seized with a panic attack just before a presentation that he had been asked to give at the clubhouse's annual transitional employment dinner. The topic was not something he was entirely comfortable speaking about in public since it recalled personal struggles that he had experienced before and after he became a member of the Club. Louis had completed two placements and was scheduled to go on a number of full-time independent job interviews. About an hour before his scheduled presentation, he started shaking. He had trouble breathing and was making incoherent sounds. Lanoil explains what happened:

> I vividly remember Louis and John coming on stage and hearing Louis make a heartfelt presentation about how mental illness had affected him and how his involvement in the Club program was helping him to regain a productive life. How did it happen, as I knew that his anxiety was high and he doubted he would be able to make his presentation, fearful of trying an activity to which he clearly sensed he was ill suited? John explained that the key to help-

ing Louis change his mind was his promise to be on stage with him, and not only to be there but to be close enough for Louis to touch him if he needed to. Before this explanation, I had wondered why John was standing in such close proximity to Louis on the stage. By using himself as an example of a person who had also experienced anxiety, John put Louis's anxiety into a normal context, which was reassuring to Louis. By virtue of his relationship (which I believe was significant), he offered the emotional support which ultimately helped Louis make his speech.

Support for taking a risk involves the combination of sound advice and the commitment just to be there and remain a close presence for the individual should he stumble.

This sense of mindful presence is reflected in another story from the same clubhouse. Here, we have Marc, the leader of an activity group, and Club member Irene:

Members started arriving at 8:30 a.m. and Irene, who had her own transportation, arrived at 11 a.m. There was a ticket system for coat retrieval which Irene understood and coordinated. Marc therefore wanted Irene to come in at 9 a.m. When approached, Irene refused, citing her long-standing inability to "get up" in the morning before 10 a.m. Marc believed that Irene could get up earlier and made his belief known to her while simultaneously expressing his need for her assistance at 9 a.m. Marc and Irene had a relatively significant relationship so that Marc's request and Irene's perceived inability to satisfy that request was upsetting to her and manifested itself in her failure to attend for three days. When Marc did reach out to her, they agreed that Marc would call her every morning at 7:45 a.m. and she would try to get up. After about a week, Irene was coming in at 9 a.m. without Marc's assistance. When I talked to Irene about this event, she explained that what motivated her to try to get up early in the morning was her belief that Marc would not reject her if she failed, and that therefore the opportunity to try reduced her stress and fear of failure. Soon after, Irene was working at a food service store that opened at 8 a.m.

The opportunity to take a risk knowing that one would not be rejected for failing is a powerful elixir. The member at once understands the importance of the task and senses the danger it poses in stretching beyond his comfort zone. In both of these stories, the motivational coach created a supportive environment marked by a mindful presence. He offered sound practical advice in how to make the leap, while affirming the value that trying is more important than failing. This supportive atmosphere pervades Fountain House and makes its culture radically different from that of the outside world.[3] Once a member trusts his or her staff worker, the significant bond between them becomes another device in the motivational coach's tool kit to engage the member in the Fountain House working community.

Ultimately, significant staff–member relationships are what make Fountain House appear to run so smoothly. Many first-time visitors to Fountain House are amazed at how effortlessly it seems to operate. Within Fountain House, however, everyone is well aware that the day moves along smoothly because of the strength of sound social relationships shared by members and staff. In essence, motivational coaches are practitioners of "social persuasion" (Bandura, 1997); they are people who are capable of assisting members without undermining their sense of self-efficacy. John Beard was an eminent practitioner of social persuasion and structured Fountain House in such a manner that all staff workers exercised this same role. He expected staff to find something of value in the members with whom they worked, and to employ their imagination in attempting to bring withdrawn individuals out of their isolation. The degree of closeness in these relationships between members and staff raises ancillary concerns regarding boundaries and dependency, which we address in chapter 7.

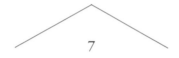

7

ISSUES IN
RELATIONSHIPS

Social workers should not take unfair advantage of any
professional relationship or exploit others to further their
personal, religious, political, or business interest.

—NATIONAL ASSOCIATION OF SOCIAL WORKERS, *CODE OF ETHICS*

Bob Jackson, a former staff worker at Fountain House and now a
retired professor of social work, once recounted an incident that he
considered illustrative of the nature of the member–staff relationship
at Fountain House. While working in the dining room at Fountain
House, he observed a member pacing back and forth, agitated and
speaking in a loud voice. A staff worker standing nearby, who was
anxious to clear the tables and reset them for the next lunch group,
tapped the member on the shoulder and asked if he would give him
some help. The member, regaining his composure, agreed and immediately proceeded to work alongside the staff worker to prepare the
dining tables for the hungry arrivals. For Jackson, the incident spoke
directly to how significant relationships that exist between members
and staff at Fountain House can have a positive impact upon behavior and open communication in situations where frequently little
exists. As discussed in chapter 6, relationships in support of recovery
hold profound implications for social practice at Fountain House.
Member-staff relationships at Fountain House foster trust and open
communications and function as a powerful tool for engaging members in the operations of the house.

At the same time, we need to be realistic about the limits within a relational intervention. Staff need to understand when recovery relationships are practicable and when they are not. They need to be familiar with the ethical issues involved, so as not to abuse the openness and vulnerability of the members. In this chapter, therefore, we will discuss how to give this powerful tool the careful attention it demands. Four issues dominate the limits and potential problems that arise from significant relationships—namely, defining the boundaries that exist in relationships; working with members who are in obvious psychosis; dealing with dependent behavior that undermines a member's autonomy and self-determination; and finally, addressing the circumstances under which members can be excluded from a working community. Throughout, we are sensitive to the fact that staff workers at Fountain House must manage the space in the coaching relationship between themselves and the members so that, while genuine and close, it always remains respectful, professional, and realistic.

Boundaries

It is not uncommon to hear members of Fountain House speak about their staff workers in demonstrative terms. The rigid social boundaries that are enforced in most social services agencies just don't seem to apply in the exchanges that occur within Fountain House. Take, for example, these excerpts from a speech by a member at an international seminar with hundreds of people in attendance; in the speech the speaker affectionately described her relationships with Fountain House social workers. The member had been institutionalized at the age of fourteen; she was twenty-seven at the time of the speech. She had no friends except her psychiatrist. She recalled:

> I remember that about a week after I got to Fountain House, a staff member took me out for coffee. Now when I was in another program and the staff worker did the same thing, she said, "If we were caught, I would be fired." So when I was having coffee with this

staff member, I was looking out the window saying, "Oh my god, she's going to get fired from Fountain House, she's going to lose her job, oh my God," but nothing happened . . .

We have a farm at Highpoint, New Jersey, where staff workers and members from Fountain House live very closely together. We cook together and clean together, and I got to see Tom in a bathrobe, which is a crummy plaid that he rescued out of a garbage can. Actually, most of his clothes are supplied by me and the thrift shop. Together we manage to keep him clothed . . .

I have a serious form of depression and I've tried to take my life many times. Usually, when I call my psychiatrist and I'm upset, he tells me to take some extra medication. But when I call Tom, he doesn't say that; he says, "India, if you should do something to yourself, I would be so devastated. You mean a lot to me."

That's all I really have to say, that he's always been there for me. It's been a moving experience. (Ely, 1992)

Such expressions do not indicate a complete lack of boundaries or a breakdown in professional ethics. Rather, the community culture of Fountain House calls for a different ethic, from which the professional derives a sense of boundaries that is distinct from the practice of distancing that is common in traditional therapeutic settings. Recovery relationships, which carry the imperative to reach out and lift the members out of their social isolation and make them feel human again, have their own proper sense of boundaries and distance. Such relationships are based on the trust and mutual respect stemming from any normal human relationship and a sense of collegiality that comes from working together on common projects.

Distance between participants is an attribute of all human relationships, including helping relationships. For example, the goal of psychoanalytic treatment is the development of a transferential relationship with a patient, which requires creating a clear boundary and distance in the relationship for the therapy to be effective. Therapists do not discuss their own problems or share information about their personal lives. Nor do they introduce their patients to their family or friends or promote after-hours socialization. Given that students of social work get a lot of training in psychoanalytic theory, they can easily develop an erroneous belief that all helping relationships require such space and boundaries. In reality this is necessary only in psychoanalytic transferential practice. Or, it may simply be that detachment is mandated by the service agency employing the social worker. Consequently, some social workers, misreading therapeutic practice, may believe that maintaining a personal distance is required in a helping relationship. Actually, most people in the helping professions who are not practicing some form of transferential therapy value closeness as a preferred spatial arrangement because it facilitates open, unimpeded conversation that promotes information gathering and maximizes the influential capacity of the helper. Thus, social workers ought to take note that, while maintaining a form of emotional distance as prescribed, they may be mistakenly separating themselves from the very people they want to help.

At Fountain House, no such prohibitions exist. In fact, staff-only or member-only spaces are prohibited. There are no "staff-only" lunchrooms or "staff-only" bathrooms, with the result that interactions between members and staff are pervasive. As social practitioners and generalists, Fountain House staff do not restrict their relationships to specific treatments. To this end, the culture of Fountain House goes to extreme lengths to foster relationships. The staff meet the members in all domains of their lives, including socially. At Fountain House (as in Rogerian client-centered models of therapy[1]), distant, detached staff are ineffective in forming the collegial, reciprocal, and caring relationships that are necessary for effective functioning as a motivational coach. This active participation of staff in building social networks creates a closeness among members and staff and facilitates a greater possibility that trusting relationships will develop. Staff attempts to facilitate participation during the workday, for example, by helping to remove impediments to recovery foster a regard for the staff person, as was illustrated in the opening story of this chapter. Fountain House has in effect operationalized the practices of Rogers within the context of a working community.

This is an openness and trust that the staff worker must not abuse. Setting limits in the familial role of motivational coach involves the clear understanding and application in practice that the focus of the relationship is on the member's, not the staff worker's, personal needs, growth, and development. Closeness in the relationship must be built on the selflessness of the service provider, which fosters trust, not exploitation. Recognizing that relationships among people are a fundamental vehicle for change implies the ethical proviso clearly stated in the social worker's Code of Ethics: "Social workers should not take unfair advantage of any professional relationship or exploit others to further their personal, religious, political, or business interests" (National Association of Social Workers, 2008). Thus staff workers at Fountain House who have a significant relationship with a member must remember that the reason for the relationship is to help the member regain the ability to relate within a group, whether as part of a functioning team at Fountain House or in an outside situation where he or she works or resides.

Moreover, staff must learn to be alert so as not to reinforce unrealistic expectations and make the motivational coach's role confusing. If the friendship issue comes up ("but aren't we friends?"), the feedback must be honest and straightforward, acknowledging the friendship while helping the member to understand the responsibilities the staff worker has in the situation—both as personal coach and as facilitator for the group. Obviously, such a close and familiar interactive environment as Fountain House can sometimes give rise to misunderstandings. Inappropriate behaviors are usually based on a variety of unrealistic expectations or beliefs, which the staff person may or may not have stimulated. Members may confuse familiarity and closeness in productive endeavors with personal affection or intimacy that steps over the line. In practice, a coach must respond immediately to any statements or actions that have sexual connotations. The response can be verbal or by gesture, but it must clearly indicate the unacceptable nature of the behavior, since too much discussion, regardless of content, can feed fantasies. Thus, while the space in motivational coaching as practiced at Fountain House may be close, its boundaries are still clear. They are the normal boundaries between any two human beings that foster mutual respect and the mutual acknowledgment of the personal limits within which an individual works.

Dealing with Psychosis

Staff workers at Fountain House come from diverse educational backgrounds. Yet, in dealing with members who are in the midst of a psychotic episode, staff are still expected to be able to recognize the seriousness of the problem and understand the steps they must take in managing it. We realize that there are times when a member can become wholly consumed by the illness. In our experience, however, there is almost always some area of sanity that can be reached by a trusted associate. If a staff person has a significant relationship with a member or can appeal to some mutual area of interest, the staff person can communicate in a reasonable manner with the member most of the time. Lanoil, for example, recounted how a staff worker who was on duty one evening at Fountain House encountered an older member, whom he knew from occasional interactions, crying in the snack bar.

> The member was sitting alone in the snack bar, distraught and tearful, and was talking aloud about incidents of being ridiculed and belittled. "I want to leave Fountain House and go into a hospital and not do anything." These remarks were followed by continual crying mixed in with a jumble of negative recollections. As the staff member approached and sat down, he recalled a story told to him by Bob Jackson [the story related at the beginning of this chapter about the staff person who distracted a distressed member by asking him to help set tables]. With this example in mind and the point of focusing the member on a concrete activity, the staff worker asked the member what he liked to do. "Draw" was the response. The staff worker then asked the member to accompany him downstairs to the living room where they could draw together. As the member drew pictures, he began to cry again and verbalize negative recollections of abuse and ridicule. The staff worker calmly but directly said, "If you don't stop crying and talking about the past, we will stop drawing and you will have to leave." "No," the member exclaimed, "I'll stop." And he did so.

This story includes a number of elements that can effectively guide staff in responding to a potential psychotic episode. First, the staff person did something with the member that was physical, easily do-able in the environment that they were in, and consistent with his temperament. A physical activity is helpful in such situations because it changes the focus of attention from troublesome thoughts to a constructive endeavor and reduces the need for words, which, in all likelihood, can become a source of confusion and additional stress in the situation. Had the member in the story responded with something that was not feasible, like "bike riding," the staff worker would have had to find a more practical diversion. Next, the staff person avoided any discussion of the past. The past is filled with historical confusion and emotional land mines. The focus of the motivational coach is on the present; it is not the coach's job to correct the past. When discussions arise, the staff person needs to control the context and have the member recall positive events and interactions. If necessary, the staff person could have brought in another staff worker or member who knew the individual to assist in the situation. Finally, the staff person was clear and direct. This was not a time to field questions or probe how the member felt, as that would only have fed into the emotional turmoil the member was experiencing. A member in a situation like this may be struggling with a process that he senses is out to destroy his very existence. Therefore, staff must focus on a process to control the situation.

In summary, then, if someone is having a psychotic episode, staff workers have a basic choice: either refocus the member on an activity or refer him to a hospital or crisis center—otherwise the intervention will require a great deal of individual attention or expertise in medication, neither of which is a course of action available to the Fountain House staff worker. As in the episode described above, the staff worker addresses the turmoil by relying on whatever relationship exists between him and the member. This intentional *use of self* in crisis situations is an appropriate role for staff and is consistent with expectations for Fountain House practice. Staff at Fountain House refocus the person through tasks, not through talk therapy. Staff need only to be adept at keeping the situation from spiraling out of control.

The aim is to keep the focus on the present and what is real, not to deal with the past or with potential delusions. Because of the relationships that have been formed at Fountain House, we believe that the member even in such situations is more likely to follow the advice of a person he trusts and to seek the help that is needed. The only other alternative is to refer the individual for hospitalization and outside medical care.

Dependency

While the concept of dependency is viewed negatively in social work (in contrast to empowerment), a more balanced opinion has emerged—namely, that in some instances client dependency can provide valuable social support (Bornstein, 1993). Dependency involves relying upon another for support or wanting that person to act on your behalf when you can do that yourself. Dependency, for example, is normal especially when a person is in dire need from sickness or catastrophic events that wipe out one's coherence and resources. At Fountain House, normal dependency occurs in staff–member relationships when the member depends on the staff worker for realistic feedback or assistance with social service benefits. Since modeling interactions are pervasive at Fountain House, members have many opportunities to observe staff as advocates and motivational coaches helping other members, and asking for help is normal. Thus, when a staff worker at Fountain House is viewed by a member as someone the member can use as a role model or when a staff coach has proven herself to be trustworthy, caring, and available to assist in many types of situations, a healthy dependency can emerge in the relationship. As a result, the motivational coaches are considered worthy of regard, which in turn allows them to provide the support and influence necessary for a member to assume responsibilities in activities or to moderate behaviors that impede forward movement and progress.

Such relationships can also create a mystique of dedication and caring, which understandably can in some cases result in a negative form of dependency—for example, wanting to work with only one staff person or being unable do anything alone without an accompanying staff person. Some members want to work only with staff and will not accept assistance from other members on the unit. Members can even become dependent on the structure of the workday, wanting to control a particular task and not letting others do work that they consider their own. Whatever the case, such instances of negative dependency prevent members from moving on with their lives or taking risks. And staff at Fountain House have to constantly judge whether a given expression of dependency is necessary at a particular moment or whether the member is losing the sense of self-efficacy and becoming dependent upon the worker for what he can do for himself. Lanoil illustrates the issue by describing the situation faced by Susan, a member in the clerical unit who had been attending Fountain House on a daily basis for about sixteen months:

> Her staff worker believed that Susan was ready for a transitional community job, but all offers to Susan met with refusal and the comment "I'm afraid and I'm not ready." Her staff worker had been helpful to Susan in many instances, especially in helping her find affordable housing in the Fountain House apartment program, and they had developed a significant relationship. Through a series of conversations with Susan, Mary Ann found out that Susan believed that if she took a placement she would lose the "good feelings," as she put it, that she experienced by being at Fountain House and that if she was away too long her worker would forget her. The staff person responded by designing a plan for Susan to move from the clerical unit to the employment unit, while retaining her same staff worker as her coach. After three months, if she decided to take a transitional job placement, the staff person would go with her for the first three days and after that would meet with her and a worker in the employment unit twice a week to discuss her work experiences on the job and on the unit. Susan agreed and successfully completed the job placement, went on to another placement and then a full time independent job, and became a powerful role model and speaker at the Fountain House employment meetings.

Susan's significant relationship with the staff worker at Fountain House initially had a strong element of dependency because it was limiting her forward movement. But by getting Susan to transfer to a new unit while remaining her coach, the staff person offered Susan a new group to relate to without rejecting her. Also, by staying involved with Susan, albeit on a less than daily basis, and helping her on the work placement, the staff worker maintained a supportive relationship. The positive experiences of relating to a new group of people plus the success she experienced in actual employment increased Susan's sense of self-efficacy in relation to her ability to manage her life apart from her staff worker and eventually permitted a more mature relationship with her worker to develop.

When you analyze dependency as a crippling issue in relationships, it is usually presented as a negative set of behaviors that, although necessary in childhood, become counterproductive in adulthood. These are people who are constantly in panic about their relationships and who need regular reassurance, which they attempt to get, for example, by calling a staff person numerous times a day. This helpless and cloying behavior is a self-defeating form of dependency that, in effect, sabotages the self-determination that relationships at Fountain House are seeking to foster. Thus when a member starts to skew a relationship by constantly and inappropriately seeking ways of gaining reassurance, realistic and non-rejecting feedback is called for. But dependency can also arrest personal development and prevent autonomy. So, when members abandon their autonomy and their responsibility for doing something for themselves and seek to cause another person to do what they themselves can do, then the staff worker needs to intervene and address the dependent behavior directly. The ultimate goal of any helping process is for the client to become more autonomous and independent, and rely on intrinsic sources of motivation and reward.

At some times Fountain House has been accused of fostering dependency as a result of a no-time-limits policy for membership. Such criticism, however, does not take into account how much time is needed to deal with mental illness. It ignores the recurring nature of the illness. Fountain House also understands that time is needed to establish trust. It is trust that makes dependency work to the benefit of the member. Trust allows members to step out of their comfort zone and take a risk because they trust that the staff will be there to support them should they trip and fall.

Limits in a Relational Approach

Glickman (1992), in his article "What If Nobody Wants to Make Lunch?," raises one of the most intractable issues faced by a working community: member choice. When a treatment assumes participant choice as integral to its effectiveness, choice plays an important role in determining membership and participation. When members choose not to attend, or if they do attend, are content to sit around and drink coffee, Fountain House has no enforcement mechanism to compel participation. Needless to say, such a situation calls for ongoing reflection and innovation regarding the effectiveness of the treatment's current programmatic structures. But it also indicates the limits in the reach and appropriateness of a working community for the entire population suffering from mental illness. The approach is limited by the choice and behavior of the target client population.

We are aware that stigma alone does not account for why members face exclusion in society. Members themselves exhibit behaviors that are deeply troubling to society. And Fountain House, as a microcosm of that society, is not exempt from making similar decisions that result in exclusion from its community. The significant trusting relationships that are formed within the workday structure at Fountain House for the most part enable members and staff to handle instances of psychiatric breakdown that outside of Fountain House normally induce fear and exclusion. Behaviors, however, that either undermine the smooth running of the house as a working community or abuse its trust are what results in disciplinary interventions. Theft, for example, which undermines the openness and trust that pervades the Fountain House culture, is treated with little tolerance. In other words, it is not the psychiatric illness that excludes members from the community. Rather, it is those attendant behaviors over which members have control that result in their exclusion. Members who arrive inebriated or high on drugs or angry and verbally abusive are asked to leave the premises, albeit on a temporary basis. Moreover, members will be required to seek appropriate counseling before readmission if the abusive behavior becomes habitual. In effect, when forced into a choice between attending to the individual or to the community, Fountain House will choose the preservation of community.

The Fountain House working community considered in isolation does not present itself as the comprehensive solution in meeting the service needs of the mental health population that society is in search of. Fountain House, however, understands that if its internal collaborative approach is replicated externally, it, along with other practitioners and concerned citizens in mental health, can begin to address the crises of regional and national community-based services for people suffering from severe mental illness. As discussed in the afterword, a recovery-oriented working community in collaboration with other agents and institutions in the community can provide one such comprehensive, cost-effective solution.

A PLACE FOR RECOVERY
IN THE COMMUNITY

> That's not the story of America. Yes, we are rugged
> individualists. Yes, we are strong and self-reliant. . . . But there's
> always been another thread running throughout our history
> —a belief that we're all connected, and that there are some
> things we can only do together as a nation.
>
> —BARACK OBAMA

> While Americans have always prized individualism,
> they've prized community just as much.
>
> —E. J. DIONNE, *OUR DIVIDED POLITICAL HEART*

The idea of having a place, like the Fountain House working community, is what is needed and missing in the community mental health system of today. Despite decades since the acceptance of the idea that people with mental illness can live in the community, society has failed to provide anything near the range and depth of services needed so that they can live in a meaningful and productive way. As mental health policymakers and practitioners strive to design such a recovery system, it is becoming clear that a strictly medical approach of hospitalization and symptom reduction no longer offers an adequate path in mental health services. Moreover, while a model employing a range of services along different dimensions of recovery is popular and includes employment, education, social functioning, and even spirituality components (Whitley & Drake, 2010), the question of how best to deliver these services and achieve the results expected still persists.

The current debate revolves around the best way to promote the social inclusion of people with mental illness within the community. One view advocates that the professional and related services be delivered directly to individuals in the community. This is known as a natural-supports or *in vivo* approach (Rapp & Goscha, 2006). In this perspective, social inclusion is a form of normalization where "individuals with disabilities live, work, play, and lead their daily lives without distinction from and with the same opportunities as individuals without disabilities" (p. 28). Consequently, proponents view any arrangement where people with disabilities associate in a place as "segregation" and as a violation of the *in vivo* ethic. In effect, promoters of a *natural supports approach* bypass traditional assembly places and community centers. Instead, they intend to exploit the individual's resilience and the natural resources of the environment to support their living within the community independently.

An alternative view, the *mutual aid approach*, which arises out of the Fountain House experience and the self-help movement (Chamberlin, Rogers, & Edison, 1996; Clay, 2005; Mowbray et al., 1988), advocates for the establishment of places in society in which people living with mental illness can meet, organize, and utilize their talents to help each other. Within this perspective Fountain House represents a collaborative recovery center where those with and without mental illness associate on a daily basis in a productive manner to support the advancement of people living with mental illness in society.[1] We suggest here that having a place like the Fountain House working community, which promotes its members' potential for psychiatric recov-

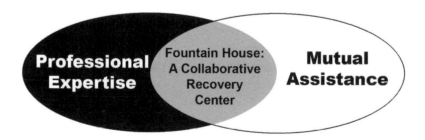

Fountain House is a collaborative recovery center that combines the expertise of the professional social worker (social practice) with the peer support (mutual assistance) of the consumer movement.

ery through the mutual assistance of the staff and members together, is what is needed in the community mental health service system of today.

Support for Recovery

Social isolation has become the number one problem that people suffering from mental illness face. Most people who are affected by mental illness tend to withdraw and isolate. The reality for many is a life of quiet desperation. As we have discussed, many formerly hospitalized patients live in society but are not really a part of it. Families understand this issue better than most professionals do because they are often the caregiver of last resort. But even families with great resources are stymied by this problem as they watch their children ending up living at home well into their adult years. We have also seen how people without purpose or meaning in their lives, and those who feel helpless, turn to drastic measures to alleviate their pain. Social isolation in the extreme can lead to suicide (Trout, 1980).

Before the last decade, the most common form of support in the community for people with serious mental illness was a once-a-week visit for therapy and a monthly medication check with a psychiatrist. Today, however, the practice of using a therapist as the main support person has been curtailed and patients simply meet with their psychiatrist once a month, usually for fifteen minutes, for medication monitoring and changes in prescription (Lehman et al., 2004). In its place some form of case management has become the rule.[2] In addition, access to community-based social and medical services is complicated by their disparate locations within a service delivery area. Clients are required to travel to a variety of locations or agencies in order to get the help they need, in effect compromising the stated objective of continuity of care in a comprehensive system. Since it is often hard for the individual client to navigate this array of services (all too often, the clients get lost in the process), the additional role of the case manager has been introduced[3] to connect clients to the disparate, uncoordinated community services. As described by Rose

(1992), "Continued fragmentation within large provider systems and across different service delivery systems characterize the setting for case management practice" (p. vii). Case management promises a continuum of care that provides comprehensive and integrated services for a population whose ability to cope is impaired in the face of such complex structural environments.

The basic formula for the case management model is similar. The nature and extent of its professional responsibilities usually consist of weekly meetings, benefits counseling, linkage to housing, and medical or psychiatric services. More recently, job placement assistance has been added to the list of services. Some case managers and their teams are expected to directly assist the client in securing benefits or an apartment, but the majority of case managers are coordinators who are expected to find others to provide this support.

Such a service system is viewed as comprehensive in design because it offers an array of programming options that are made available to the client on the basis of an assessment of his or her needs. For the most part, these initiatives also follow an individualized service system approach (described in chapter 3), which features focused roles for individual professionals who are expected to provide a service to the client or patient. Such an approach is considered to be characteristically American in design. Time-limited, discrete services reflect the American ideal of rugged individualism (Hofstadter, 1944) as applied to social welfare. As Lamb (1994) noted in comparing American and British mental health community support systems, "Americans emphasize skills acquisition and the importance of a skills based approach in helping people function as independent as possible with the minimum of support" (p. 1019). Such a system is premised on the belief that once one or more of these interventions are successfully completed, be it therapy or supported employment, the individual is expected to have successfully recovered and to be ready to launch into independence in the community. In Great Britain, on the other hand, skills acquisition tends to take second place to helping people adapt to their circumstances. Our solution, the working community, is an empowerment strategy—not just a "fix it" strategy—that embraces the involvement of our members in their own recovery.

Many of these programs also advocate an *in vivo* or natural supports arrangement. Their premise is that once a person is living independently in the community, sufficient non–mental health supports can be found to offer a variety of opportunities or "natural supports." With this understanding in mind, caseworkers are expected to help their clients access the resources in the larger community that will support them on their road to recovery. Such programs further assume that the larger community is welcoming to people suffering from mental illness and is relatively free of stigma.

There is little evidence to suggest, however, that this is what actually occurs for the majority of people living in the community. While the approach appears on its surface to give people a certain level of independence, it can just as often leave them to fend for themselves. Actually there is an alternative view of contemporary society that the potential for supporting *in vivo* reintegration efforts is disappearing (Putnam, 2000). For the members of Fountain House, as well as for people anywhere suffering from mental illness, society can still be a hostile environment. The stigma against people with mental illness is strong and real in many facets of the larger world, whether it is present on the job, at school, in an apartment, or in a restaurant. An example of the dilemma faced by people living with mental illness is how disquieting the issue of self-disclosure is for students returning to school (Dougherty et al., 1996).[4] Most people choose not to disclose their mental health issues to their employer, and many are reluctant to tell their boyfriend or girlfriend about their mental health condition. Our members live in the real world, not an idealized one. In reality, people with serious mental illness have daily encounters with various forms of stigma that cause them to be viewed with both fear and suspicion. In our future idealized world, we may eliminate stigma, but in today's world, having a safe, accepting place to freely be themselves is a crucial part of recovery.

It is equally true that many people with mental illness have behaviors that are often misunderstood by those in the larger community. In the real world, bizarre behavior or emotional rage in public can easily lead to trouble with the police, which is why so many people with mental illness end up in jail. To build an effective support system there has to be recognition of the realities of these negative behaviors and the resulting trouble that people with mental illness find themselves in. In place of a focus on individual human deficiencies, however, Fountain House approaches the problem more holistically—as the attendant consequences of social isolation and an expression of the need for niches of human company for support—and suggests that there be a place where people living with mental illness can gather to overcome their sense of isolation and find meaning in their lives and a circle of friends for support.

Peer Support Initiatives

One positive direction in community mental health services that supports this view has been the development of peer support programs (Clay, 2005; Solomon, 2004). Peer support programs operate community resource centers that sponsor various self-help initiatives, attempting to create supportive social networks among adults with mental illness. These programs view peer-operated resource programs and peer advocacy as the future base of support for ex-patients living in the community. The evidence for these approaches is still limited, but it is demonstrating constructive effects in psychiatric recovery, particularly in its use of peers as a strategic resource in a mental health team.[5] In a related vein, Mandiberg (2010, 2012) has advocated a shift in focus from professional services to a community development perspective that offers the potential for social inclusion through businesses owned and operated by people in recovery and their organizations.

Fountain House, an early proponent of mutual aid in supporting member recovery (Anderson, 1998), and the clubhouses that follow its example continue to foster a socially supportive network of professionals and peers (Carolan et al., 2011; Waegemakers Schiff, Colman, & Miner, 2008). Consequently, we suggest a different approach, especially considering all the individuals who do not benefit from the dominant individualized service system approach and the number of existing programs that overlook the impact of social isolation upon those living with mental illness in the community. It holds the additional advantage of cost-effectiveness, as studies have shown that the costs associated with working communities, where services are provided by members and staff working side by side, are one-half to one-third of those incurred in traditional professionally operated treatment programs (McKay, Yates, & Johnsen, 2007).

Collaborative Recovery Center

The Fountain House working community (i.e., a collaborative recovery center) clearly comes out of a communitarian tradition in American society (Hofstadter, 1944) in which living in a community derives an attendant sense of relatedness and social responsibility. Living in community is more than location. As discussed earlier, community is relational and involves the sense that I as a person am an integral part of a larger event (Sarason, 1974). Truly living in community is to have a "place" in that community where one takes part in its movements and gets recognized as an integral contributor. Place therefore is an important component of the social needs of every human being, but most especially among Fountain House members, many of whom have lost their place in this world.

The fact that Fountain House is established in a place does not mean it projects an institutional approach. It is in the nature of a place, as opposed to a location, to establish a defining presence for patients and clients. In an individualized service system approach, there is no "place" for people to come to. Mancini (2006), for example, reports narratives by people from the consumer movement who speak about an entirely different experience of *place* where they "were isolated in negative environments that reinforced the message that they were sick, fragile, and incompetent. They were bombarded with diagnostic labels that reinforced their identities as 'mental patient.' This resulted in an overwhelming sense of despair. . . . These messages were effectively communicated via professionals and systems that were coercive, paternal, and indifferent" (p. 17).

At Fountain House, in contrast, being a member of a community means members have a place to go where they do not have to be subjected to stigma on a day-to-day basis. Just as other groups, such as immigrants, do (Mandiberg, 2010), people with mental illness rely upon social networks to support their successful inclusion in society (Carolan et al., 2011). Or, as Beard (1978) once described, people need a place where they are "needed, expected. They have to be missed. They have to have people to give news to, good and bad. They have to have people to tell their secrets to. It's a terrible thing to have a secret and no one to tell it to" (p. 18).

In providing a place in community where members come to regain their personhood, find meaning, and be among a socially supportive group of friends and associates, Fountain House has consistently related a positive narrative concerning the treatment of people with mental illness. Many members, when they first arrive at Fountain House, do not have any clear goals. We understand that the person, at the moment that is right for him or her, will take the first step toward making a contribution and beginning reentry to the community. Sometimes the motivation comes from a big thing like a job or an apartment. But it can just as easily come from going to a baseball game or cleaning a dish. It is never certain which activity or event will trigger the first steps, but it is the sense of being needed that is the key to motivation. The gradual participation in the community and the momentum of those activities build motivation to work on individual goals. Also, having fellow travelers, other members as peers to share the experience, is as crucial in recovery as having a caring staff professional.

Practically, having a place of one's own that is both part of and separate from the larger society allows our members to come and go with ease on a daily basis, playing whatever role they wish in the society at large and returning when necessary for nurturing and reinforcement, only to return again to the larger world. With the working community adding backup and support, every member is encouraged to balance his time between our working community and the larger society. Walter, a longtime member, came to Fountain House as a young man. He left to go to work for Con Edison for twenty years, but he kept up his connection and returned upon his retirement. He now gives back to his community of choice, Fountain House. Thus moving between a world full of stigma and a place that tries to minimize it, we build the personal strength necessary to succeed. In fact, members describe Fountain House as "a place to come, a right to meaningful work, a right to meaningful relationships, a right to a place to return."[6] Thus, it is out of a sense of *place* and its attendant values for social networking within society that our working community approach was born.

We are often asked whether by creating a meaningful and caring environment we are holding people back from moving on with their lives. Annual enrollments indicate that most members, in fact, do move on; most stay only one or two years at Fountain House (but they do come back to visit). Irrespective of how long members stay, they all have the right to long-term support and the ability to access available resources in a variety of ways. We have learned through our practice that having a place to come to and a place to return to is crucial for everyone, but particularly for a group of people who often find themselves socially isolated. Our members have lost these connections—or more likely, have some support but not enough to thrive. As Ronald, a member of Fountain House and a staunch Baptist, explained: "The church people try but they just don't understand people with mental illness." Or, as Michael, a member of Fountain House who served as a board member and a placement manager in the supported-employment unit, stated, "I am not hiding from the world at Fountain House; I am helping to make the world a better place."

In a working community, the place is constructed to foster the association of people with and without mental illness, in a collaborative manner that supports member recovery. Our sixty years of practice show that an effective non-exploitive environment can be successfully created. If we cannot create places in the mental health system for this integration, what hope will we have for achieving it in the larger society? Our working community operates in the space between the mental health service system and the larger society. Unlike sheltered environments or the asylums of long ago, working communities have open borders; they are porous to the larger world while maintaining a clear skeletal system of support. In this way, our working community is an "emergent community" (Lewin, 1992), serving as a portal for our members that encourages movement and growth into the larger community. Having a place to come to and return to is crucial to the recovery of our membership. Having these working communities throughout a geographic area will provide a different kind of intervention to support people with mental illness and provide them with the services they need, such as employment and housing. They reflect a self-energizing community that works for the recovery of all its members. Consequently, we have consciously chosen to raise half of our funding from private sources in order to further connect our membership to the larger society.

Partnerships in Comprehensive Community Support

Fountain House has always projected a comprehensive approach for people with serious mental illness in the same vein as a community mental health center. While we have always recognized that the biological issues of mental health and mental illness are real and will not be fixed solely by environmental interventions,[7] we find the opposite view to be equally true, that these problems will not be fixed by clinical interventions alone, be they medication, therapy, or some other medical intervention. Denying the reality of the clinical nature of the problems does not serve our membership well, but it is also true that not being aware and not factoring in a person's day-to-day life are equally shortsighted. Recovery in society (i.e., the definition of recovery in mental health) means acknowledging that there is something real and unique about the mental health issues that people face. At the same time, Fountain House was founded before the remedy offered by medication existed; it was posited upon a belief in the fundamental resiliency of the human spirit, and we continue to operate on that belief to this day. But to achieve the goal of successful integration in society, Fountain House has always recognized the complexity of the problem and that partnerships with other agents within society are necessary. Foremost has been its partnerships with employers (i.e., through transitional employment) and its partnership with community psychiatry.

Over the last fifteen years, Fountain House has been developing a community-based recovery approach that partners its working community concept with a health service center (the Sidney Baer Center), including psychiatric services. The center is designed to provide comprehensive community support for people with mental illness to live in society (Aquila et al., 1999). Given the high incidence of serious physical health issues afflicting those with mental illness, current research has emphasized combining psychiatry with general health services (Parks et al., 2006). Fountain House has taken this concept one step further by adding a working community. The resulting amalgam of medical and psychiatric resources in concert with a working community creates a team of people focused on the recovery of the patient/member.

Such an alliance addresses the limitations of a strictly therapeutic relationship of brief encounters that focus solely on the symptoms of the illness with only partial information available for diagnostic purposes. In its place, the "rehabilitation alliance" has come to add significant value to the process of recovery by introducing both the member and his or her staff worker as active agents in the process. Both the medical and psychiatric staff and the social practitioner appreciate the subtlety of the role that choice plays in the recovery process. At their discretion, members invite their staff worker from the clubhouse or residence (or any other house member, friend, or family member) to accompany them to the storefront clinic. The social practitioner and others who have spent a great deal of time with the member are in a position to provide insight to the doctors about the unique reasons why, for example, someone is not taking his or her medicine or is facing difficulties in handling ordinary functions. Additionally, such an alliance structure broadens the scope of any inquiry so that the whole team views the goals of employment, health, housing, and education as vital to the long-term well-being of the member. In concert with establishment of the Baer Center, Fountain House has also added a wellness unit (the Lewis Wellness Center) to its basic house operation to emphasize the crucial role that diet and exercise play in the recovery of someone with serious mental illness. Consequently, the alliance has resulted in the timely detection and treatment of major medical conditions, such as diabetes and heart disease, and in a yearly rehospitalization rate of less than 10 percent.

Fountain House has also found that it is difficult to attract psychiatrists and general practitioners to work in the community with people with major mental illness. The absence of an adequate funding stream limits any ability to effectively practice. Fountain House, on the other hand, is constantly trying to create a satisfying job for the psychiatrist and facilitating long-term relationships between the doctor and the members, especially within a recovery emphasis. Our storefront psychiatrists and general practitioners have in effect a different kind of health care practice, one in which physicians resemble more the old-fashioned general practitioner whose knowledge of his patients' lives informs their treatment, or in our case, their recovery process. Each of our doctors is able to spend more than the standard fifteen-minute appointment with patients and is attuned as well to patients' recovery goals, such as jobs, school, or housing, as well as physical health. The extra time available to the psychiatrist in working with the member and the staff person ensures that there are no confounding factors to impede progress.

Our hope is that a network of these working communities in conjunction with medical and psychiatric recovery clinics will spring up to provide the combination of medical and social support necessary for a person with major mental illness to survive and thrive in today's world.

Fountain House's beginnings predated the advent of psychopharmacology and deinstitutionalization. Even so, Fountain House began with a belief in the resiliency of the human spirit and the need for a place in the community where its vision for a better life for those living with mental illness can be realized.

We have argued throughout this book that the continuity and success of Fountain House are ultimately founded on the social nature of its enterprise. Fountain House is a community of people who work side by side in support of the psychiatric recovery of its members. As such, it incorporates methodologies that have long been staples of both psychiatry and social work: task-group methodologies that offer purposeful opportunities and diverse, meaningful roles; a mutual aid framework commonly employed by immigrant and afflicted populations; and the public advocacy of the settlement house movement. Our methodology integrates the professional expertise of the social practitioner with the ideals of social justice, human respect, and member empowerment, which inspires both professional and volunteer alike. Adapting and integrating these strains of practice through innovation and reflection, Fountain House has evolved a signature approach in psychiatric recovery—the working community—that is highly transportable, cost-effective, and capable of adoption the world over.

Fountain House appreciates the deep sense of isolation suffered by people with mental illness. Our goal is the social inclusion of people who are excluded from the larger society. It is a goal that is shared by today's mental health establishment. We have, however, resisted the narrow boundaries of that establishment's strategies and suggested instead a more expansive approach. Fountain House presents the tradition and benefit of community—largely either ignored or jettisoned by the mental health establishment—that is founded in humanistic and progressive thought. Like those in the post–civil rights era, we understand that the passage of laws and the affirmation of rights, while honorable acts, are insufficient for realizing the dream of participation in society by people living with mental illness. We applaud the consumer movement and demand with it that there be places in society to bridge the chasm between the mental health service system and the larger society. An emergent working community, one that functions like a sturdy bridge, can span the chasm between the chaos of the world and the cocoon of the mental health care system and constantly support the forays of its members into the larger society. Working communities in society give members the time and space they need to explore and understand what it means to live a full life, with communities like Fountain House continuing to develop innovative techniques that support these efforts. Additionally, its collaborative nature means that it can gather the diverse interests of various public agents and stakeholders (business and health sectors in particular) with whom it forms pragmatic partnerships to provide as comprehensive a community of care as a society is able to devise. We hope that in explicating the theoretical underpinnings of our unique form of social practice, this book will encourage interest and discussion in the greater application of the working community in achieving our common vision that people with serious mental illness can live and thrive in our communities.

ACKNOWLEDGMENTS

The inception of this book dates back more than a decade, to when Alan Doyle, one of its authors, attended a lecture by Rudyard Propst, the former director of education and training at Fountain House. Every two years, followers of the Fountain House approach from all over the world meet to discuss practice and its related principles. Propst, one of the major spokespersons at the conference, made the point that John Beard was his mentor and the source for everything that he understood was associated with Fountain House. However, throughout the conference, Propst's comment was the only public reference to a man who had apparently played such a formative role in the origins of the movement. Obviously there was a need to explore Beard's influence further, and as a result Kenneth Dudek, who was the executive director of Fountain House at the time (and another author of this book), asked Stephen Anderson, a Fountain House staff member, to investigate the role of John Beard's ideas in the formation of Fountain House. Anderson was the natural choice for the inquiry, since he had already published a history of Fountain House and its influence upon the broader clubhouse movement, *We Are Not Alone* (1996).

In the midst of Anderson's research (Anderson, 2005), we realized that Fountain House was not the result of the solitary thinking of

John Beard, but reflected broader social and psychiatric movements of the time. In January 2008 Fountain House hosted a colloquium of practitioners and researchers to pursue further the question of its conceptual foundations. In the discussions that took place, two practice models emerged: one that reflected a person-in-environment approach that emphasized transforming social structures and another that focused on shaping the quality of the interpersonal relationships among members and staff. Julius Lanoil (the third author of this book, who had served as Fountain House's program director under John Beard in the 1960s and 1970s) noted in the discussions how practice today at Fountain House reflected exemplary contemporary approaches in the helping relationship. He was invited to join in the task of formulating a unified intellectual framework for the nature and practice of Fountain House.

Many people have contributed ideas to this volume throughout the years of its formulation, and several merit public recognition. The research of Stephen Anderson into the history of Fountain House is reflected throughout chapter 2. Elliott Madison, a colleague at Fountain House, acted as the conceptual midwife to this undertaking in formulating a coherent framework for the concept of community, and Jeffrey Aron, another Fountain House colleague, kept us honest in our language. Howard Owens, MD, a member of the Fountain House board of directors, advised us on technical issues related to mental illness. We also want to acknowledge James Mandiberg, assistant professor of social work at Columbia University, who advised us on directions to take; Pauline Nicholls for her international perspective and support; editors Jacquelyn Ardam, Anna Jarachowski, and Jacques Engelstein and copyeditor Jan McInroy, who variously smoothed out our prose and verified facts and citations. Seri Doyle and Barbara Lanoil were there with encouragement throughout. We are appreciative of our senior executive editors at Columbia University Press, initially Lauren Dockett and now Jennifer Perillo, who unfailingly believed in our project and provided guidance throughout the process.

Finally, this book would never have been written if it were not for the courage of the members of Fountain House, who for more than sixty years have demonstrated their loyalty and commitment to maintaining its existence as a crucial element in restoring meaning and accomplishment to their lives and to the lives of others who suffer from mental illness. The membership of the Fountain House community is the single motivating factor for the continued existence of Fountain House and the living proof of its effectiveness. This sentiment was expressed by one of the very first members of Fountain House, Michael Obolensky, in a 1943 letter to Elizabeth Schermerhorn, the creator of the Fountain House Foundation. Obolensky implored his long-standing patron from Rockland State Hospital with the words "do not give up on us." *Fountain House*, the book, is another chapter in keeping our promise not to give up on our membership.

CHRONOLOGY

1944   The first official meeting of WANA (the We Are Not Alone Society) is held at the Third Street YMCA in Manhattan. The meeting grew out of a self-help group that originated at Rockland State Hospital. It was organized by Michael Obolensky, a former patient, and Elizabeth Schermerhorn, a volunteer. Ten members and Mrs. Schermerhorn were present.

1947   WANA declines and the need for reorganization becomes clear. Concerns revolve around the group's administrative instability and the need for a building of its own.

1948   Elizabeth Schermerhorn and her friend Hetty Hemenway Richard locate a brownstone for sale at 412 West 47th Street.

1948   The Fountain House Foundation is incorporated with a five-member board of directors, including Mrs. Schermerhorn and Mrs. Richard. The Fountain House Fellowship, comprising exclusively former patients, is established separately but under the auspices of the foundation. The Fellowship mainly provides social and recreational activities in the evenings and on weekends.

1955   John Beard, an innovative social worker from Michigan, is named executive director. He immediately engages unemployed members in working with him to fix up the building during the daytime.

1956   The Fountain House Fellowship is dissolved. All members are invited to rejoin Fountain House as a single organization.

1957   Fountain House is registered as a service trademark with the U.S. Patent Office.

1958 The first assignments of the employment placement project, later known as transitional employment, are secured.

1958 Fountain House begins to secure leases for apartments in the community. Board member Hetty Richard personally signs many of these leases.

1959 The National Institute of Mental Health awards Fountain House a grant for a two-year research study comparing people accepted into the day program with people denied Fountain House services. Results of the study show a 30 percent reduction in rehospitalization of Fountain House members.

1965 The new building at 425 West 47th Street is dedicated.

1974 Fountain House purchases six brownstones to the west of the main building. Two of these are converted into the Ellabee Guesthouse to house colleagues attending training at Fountain House.

1975 The High Point Farm in Montague, New Jersey, is bequeathed to the organization by Karl Keller, a former board member.

1976 The snack bar and mezzanine are added to serve as the youth center. The first Fountain House young adult program begins.

1976 Fountain House is awarded a multi-year grant from the National Institute of Mental Health to establish a national training program to teach the model to community-based organizations.

1981 The first international seminar is held in Lahore, Pakistan, organized by Dr. M. R. Chaudhry.

1982 John Beard dies after a two-and-a-half-year battle with lung cancer. James Schmidt assumes the position of executive director.

1984 Fountain House opens the residence at 441 West 47th Street. It is the first HUD-funded mental health residence in the country.

1985 The four brownstones next to Fountain House are renovated and dedicated as the van Ameringen Center.

1989 The Standards for Clubhouse Development are adopted after lengthy debate and discussion across the entire clubhouse movement. The standards outline the guiding principles of a Fountain House community.

1992 The Storefront, an off-site office where members can receive psychiatric and primary medical care, opens in partnership with St. Luke's–Roosevelt Medical Center.

1992 Kenneth Dudek is named executive director.

1994 The International Center for Clubhouse Development is created.

2000 The Fountain Gallery opens.

2003 The first annual luncheon symposium takes place at the Yale Club.

2011 The Lewis Wellness Unit is opened at Fountain House.

2011 Fountain House and St. Luke's–Roosevelt Hospital open the Sidney Baer Center, a recovery facility integrating physical and behavioral health and wellness for Fountain House members.

GLOSSARY

Fountain House introduces new language to capture the dynamics of its practice in support of the recovery of people living with mental illness. Some terms, such as *working community* and *social practice*, represent newly minted illustrative descriptions of our signature approach to social work. We include here a glossary of these terms as a preliminary reference for readers.

Activity Group Therapy (AGT): Treatment approach practiced by John Beard and colleagues at Wayne County General Hospital in the early 1950s in which patients were encouraged to participate in ordinary group activities (for example, playing catch, performing dramatic readings) as a way of recovering from mental illness.

club: Term first used by Fountain House to describe itself. Its original function and activities were modeled after social clubs of the 1950s.

clubhouse: Term commonly used by programs that claim to be modeled after Fountain House (some of which bear no resemblance to the model presented in this book). We prefer the term *working community* to describe the Fountain House approach.

Eloise: Nickname for Wayne County General Hospital, located outside Detroit, where John Beard, as a graduate student doing his field placement in social work, learned Activity Group Therapy.

member: Term applied to participants of Fountain House, rather than *patients* or *clients*, in recognition of their constitutive role in the operation of the working community.

milieu therapy: A therapeutic approach in mental health common in the mid-twentieth century that expected everyone who came in contact with the patient (i.e., the patient's social milieu), to contribute in the patient's recovery.

motivational coaching: Aspect of social practice that focuses on staff forming one-on-one supportive relationships with members at Fountain House.

recovery: Current paradigm in mental health that affirms that people suffering from mental illness can lead satisfying and productive lives in society despite their illness.

social practice: Approach to practice at Fountain House that promotes member participation in task-group activities and the formation of the working community.

standards: A series of practices developed in 1989 by Fountain House together with other established clubhouses across the world that defined the essential framework of the Fountain House approach.

transformational design: Aspect of social practice that arranges the social structure of Fountain House as a humane, strengths-based, and empowering place for members to make their own contributions to the community.

WANA (We Are Not Alone) Society: The precursor organization to Fountain House that was formed in the mid-1940s by a group of ex-patients from Rockland State Hospital and their wealthy advocates to provide support to those leaving the hospital in finding housing and jobs and to foster social activities.

working community: Term used to describe the nature of Fountain House and its methodology for the recovery and social inclusion of people suffering from mental illness.

NOTES

Introduction

1. The reference is listed as the ICCD Clubhouse Model with Fountain House as its source. In 1994 Fountain House formed the International Center for Clubhouse Development (ICCD) to assume responsibility for building and coordinating a network of programs modeled after its innovative insights.

2. *Traitement moral*, or the *moral treatment*, was a psychological treatment for people suffering from mental illness developed by the renowned French physician Philippe Pinel in the late eighteenth century. It emphasized therapeutic observations and discussions and an environment that was conducive to a humane, caring approach.

3. *Deinstitutionalization* refers to the large-scale discharge of people with severe mental illness back into the community, emphasizing least-restrictive treatment settings (Rosenberg & Rosenberg, 2006).

4. Under the rehabilitation option of the federal Medicaid program—Social Security Act, Sec. 1905(a)(13)—states may choose to offer to reimburse nonmedical treatments such as schooling and job development.

5. See discussion on the Fountain House recovery center concept, the Sidney Baer Center, in the afterword.

6. There are currently more than 340 clubhouses, located on every continent, that claim to faithfully follow the Fountain House model (International Center for Clubhouse Development, 2012).

7. Particularly Jackson's textbook (2001), *The Clubhouse Model*, which explores the structure of clubhouses as a case study for learning generalist

social work practice, and Mandiberg's (2000) doctoral dissertation, which focuses on factors affecting the spread of the model. Aside from the rare acknowledgment of the formative historical role played by Fountain House in most of today's psychiatric rehabilitation programs (Sowbel & Starnes, 2006, p. 25), Fountain House receives only perfunctory mention in social work textbooks and rarely, if ever, appears as a conventional model for study in contemporary mental health theory and practice in schools of social work.

8. The term *working community*, rather than the word *clubhouse*, is used by Fountain House to describe its signature approach to psychiatric recovery. To many, "clubhouse" is synonymous with Fountain House, and there are a number of excellent programs that use this description to identify themselves. Unfortunately, over the intervening decades of the term's use, a number of programs have adopted it for a wide variety of practices, creating many misconceptions about our approach. Fountain House is adopting the term "working community" as the generic name for its approach to avoid the confusion that has developed with regard to the meaning of the word "clubhouse."

9. *Transitional employment* is a temporary job placement invented by Fountain House that supports the social inclusion of its members; it is more fully described in chapter 2.

1. Insights from Activity Group Therapy

1. This practice of recruiting former patients in the operation of the hospital was similar to the approach, eventually adopted by Beard, of involving members in the operation of Fountain House.

2. Early installations included the McLean Asylum (today the noted McLean Hospital), the Bloomingdale Asylum (the first asylum for the care of the mentally ill in New York City, which subsequently sold part of its lands for the present-day Columbia University in Morningside Heights), and an asylum opened by the Society of Friends in Frankford, Pennsylvania, outside of Philadelphia, which was modeled on the York Retreat.

3. Chapter 2 will return to this aspect of AGT in understanding Beard's rejection of the member-run Fellowship at Fountain House, which was based on an opposing, separatist vision that is common even today among some consumer groups (Borkman, 1999).

2. Reinventing Fountain House

1. The authors are indebted to Professor James Mandiberg of Columbia University for this insight.

2. Beard would argue, for example, that children's play is really work. He explained, "You watch them play. They have a lot more pain than we do in our lives when they go out to play. They physically get hurt. They're struggling with relationships. They really like to think they're playing. I think they're working and they're learning. And they are trying to manipulate and control and achieve. And there is a feeling of product, no matter what they are doing, in the simplest of games in the sense of accomplishment. That's what we all do" (Beard, 1978).

3. In recent years, the authors have come to understand that having an independent board of directors is crucial to creating an effective Fountain House program. Clubhouses incorporated within broader mental health agencies seem to come and go; without an independent board of directors, no structural exigency exists for maintaining the program, especially once the initial committed staff move on in their careers.

4. Figures do not include the number of staff assigned to an extensive housing program operated by Fountain House.

5. The section on societal integration has been adapted from an unpublished manuscript by Stephen Anderson (2005) on the role of John Beard in shaping practice at Fountain House.

6. Today TE situations are designed to last for six to nine months.

7. Keller would years later donate a farm located in northern New Jersey to Fountain House, known as the High Point Farm.

8. No staff lived in these apartments. All support was provided by staff based at Fountain House. These apartments represented one of the earliest versions of *supported housing* (Hogan & Carling, 1992).

3. Core Principles of a Working Community

1. See standard 15: "The work-ordered day engages members and staff together, side-by-side, in the running of the Clubhouse" (International Center for Clubhouse Development, 2012, p. 18).

2. Adherents of Sarason who promote the understanding of the psychological sense of community (McMillan & Chavis, 1986) have since gone on to seek ways to detect and quantify its impact. Glynn's work (1981) here is particularly relevant, since it demonstrates the relationship between the sense of community and an individual's ability to function competently within it.

3. "Total push" is a term used at the time to designate a program to facilitate the capacity of patients for improved socialization (Greenblatt, York, & Brown, 1955, p. 357).

4. Fountain House restricts its membership to those individuals with the diagnoses of schizophrenia, bipolar illness, and major depression. Eligibility restrictions are a matter of expediency, and not an essential treatment

principle. Resource husbandry requires limits on the number of members that can be served at any one time. Thus, while Fountain House considers its design universal in application, it limits the actual application of it to a manageable target population. It is left to others to determine its broader adoption.

5. Fountain House hires staff who hold the professional degree of master's in social work (MSW), or graduate degrees in other fields, such as education, employment, anthropology, philosophy, sociology, and counseling.

6. Typically, strategies utilized by normative organizations involve participation, feedback including evaluation and follow-up, social awareness, and education. As Etzioni (1961) explained: "Compliance in normative organization rests principally on internalization of directives accepted as legitimate; leadership and manipulation of social and prestige symbols and socialization are among the more important techniques of control used" (p. 366). Since these strategies are all employed by Fountain House, some might label Fountain House as a purely normative organization that utilizes its moral power to achieve social compliance and a high level of involvement among its participants. The problem with such an inference is its implication of member submission to staff power and their directives. The prevalence of choice throughout the membership of a working community disrupts submissive relationships. In a sense, Fountain House represents a hybrid of normative and social exchange types of organization, in which power and relationships are defined as growing out of face-to-face involvement. In such an organization, as illustrated by Fountain House, the staff's need to control is quieted and peer relationships are pervasive.

4. Defining Social Practice

1. The authors are indebted to Marianne Kristiansen (2006) for the term *social practice* to characterize the professional methodology described in this book.

5. Transformational Design

1. "Through the persuasive power of numbers, multiplicity of modeling augments the strength of vicarious experience" (Bandura, 1997, p. 99).

6. Motivational Coaching

1. *Negative symptoms* refers to the weakening or lack of normal thoughts, emotions, or behavior particularly associated with patients suffering from schizophrenia. Studies of schizophrenia, for example, suggest that the treatment of negative symptoms like poor motivation, reduced affect, social withdrawal, and slowed speech and movement should be identified as a "vital clinical need." And, the authors conclude, "while more work on psychosocial treatments that specifically target negative symptoms is necessary, referral to psychosocial treatment is an important option for physicians to consider in dealing with enduring negative symptoms" (Velligan & Alphs, 2008, p. 4).

2. It should be noted that current data at Fountain House corroborate the basic soundness of the intervention: the simultaneous encouragement to participate in Fountain House and attend school. Data collected on members (Madison & Maltz, 2012) confirm that members who continue to attend Fountain House regularly while in school are more likely to succeed academically.

3. The current practice of relying solely on natural supports in the community (*in vivo*) to effect social integration will be discussed more fully in the afterword.

7. Issues in Relationships

1. The unconditional positive regard and empathic understanding used by the Rogerian counselor contrasts with the psychoanalytic use of transference. That is because the characteristics of neutrality and emotional detachment, required by a psychoanalytic therapist in order for the transference feelings to be activated, are incompatible with Rogerian emotional expression, warmth, and acceptance (Brown & Pedder, 1991; Kahn, 1985).

Afterword: A Place for Recovery in the Community

1. If one were to locate the position of Fountain House on a continuum of services based on the source of aid in recovery—from professional to peer support—Fountain House would represent an amalgam of the two approaches, with staff assuming the expertise of social practitioners who promote mutual aid of the membership within a community working for the recovery of its members.

2. Or lately "care management," an insurance program within a restricted network of doctors and services that promises effective care at less cost.

3. In the United States, the services of case management are mandated by federal law P.L. 99–660.

4. Dougherty et al. also note the crucial need for primary support groups in helping individuals to manage such situations.

5. See Beeble & Salem, 2009; Corrigan et al., 2002, 2005; Pistrang, Barker, & Humphreys, 2008; Roberts et al., 1999; Verhaeghe, Bracke, & Bruynooghe, 2008.

6. The statement is prominently displayed at Fountain House, as well as at clubhouses around the world that imitate its methodology.

7. In fact, recognizing the importance of allied quality psychiatric care for people suffering from mental illness, Fountain House has always partnered with psychiatrists for assistance on clinical issues (Doyle, 2012).

REFERENCES

Addams, J. (1961). *Twenty years at Hull House*. New York: Penguin Putnam.

Alderfer, C. P. (1972). *Existence, relatedness, and growth*. New York: Free Press.

Anderson, P. (2005). *Stories of hope* (video). New York: International Center for Clubhouse Development.

Anderson, S. B. (1985). *The role of staff at Fountain House*. Paper presented at the Third International Clubhouse Seminar. New York: Fountain House.

———. (1998). *We Are Not Alone: Fountain House and the development of the clubhouse culture*. New York: Fountain House.

———. (2005). *John Beard: A fierce visionary*. Unpublished manuscript. New York: Fountain House.

Anthony, W. A. (1993). Recovery from mental illness: The guiding vision of the mental health service system in the 1990's. *Psychosocial Rehabilitation Journal, 16*(4), 11–23.

———. (2000). A recovery-oriented service system: Setting some system-level standards. *Psychosocial Rehabilitation Journal, 24*(2), 159–168.

Anthony, W. A., & Liberman, R. P. (1986). The practice of psychiatric rehabilitation: Historical, conceptual, and research base. *Schizophrenia Bulletin, 12*(4), 542–559.

Aquila, R., Santos, G., Malamud, T. J., & McGrory, D. (1999). The rehabilitation alliance in practice: The clubhouse connection. *Psychiatric Rehabilitation Journal, 23*(1), 19–23.

Argyris, C., Putnam, R., & Smith, D. (1985). *Action science: Concepts, methods, and skills for research and intervention*. San Francisco: Jossey-Bass.

Augé, M. (1995). *Non-places: Introduction to an anthropology of supermodernity* (J. Howe, Trans.). London: Verso.

Bandura, A. (1978). The self system in reciprocal determinism. *American Psychologist, 33*(4), 344–358.

———. (1989). Human agency in social cognitive theory. *American Psychologist, 44*(9), 1175–1184.

———. (1997). *Self-efficacy: The exercise of control.* New York: W. H. Freeman & Company.

Bartlett, H. M. (2003). Working definition of social work practice. *Research on social work practice, 13*(3), 267–270. Reprinted from H. Bartlett, (1958), Working definition of social work practice, *Social Work, 3*(2), 5–8.

Baylis, N. (2004). Teaching positive psychology. In P. A. Linley & H. Josepy (Eds.), *Positive psychology in practice* (pp. 210–217). Hoboken, NJ: John Wiley & Sons.

Beard, J. H. (1978). *Beard unplugged.* Transcript of videotape. New York: Fountain House.

Beard, J. H., Goertzel, V., & Pearce, A. J. (1958). The effectiveness of Activity Group Therapy with chronically regressed adult schizophrenics. *International Journal of Group Psychotherapy, 8*(2), 123–136.

Beard, J. H., Propst, R. N., & Malamud, T. (1982). "The Fountain House model of psychiatric rehabilitation." *Psychosocial Rehabilitation Journal, 5*(1), 47–53.

Beard, J. H., Schmidt, J., & Smith, M. M. (1963). The use of transitional employment in the rehabilitation of the psychiatric patient. *Journal of Nervous and Mental Disease, 136*(5), 507–514.

Beeble, M. L., & Salem, D. A. (2009). Understanding the phases of recovery from serious mental illness: The roles of referent and expert power in a mutual-help setting. *Journal of Community Psychology, 37*(2), 249–267.

Biddle, B. J. (1986). Recent development in role theory. *Annual Review of Sociology, 12*, 67–92.

Booth, F., Gordon, S., Carlson, C., & Hamilton, M. (2000). Waging war on modern chronic diseases: Primary prevention through exercise biology. *Journal of Applied Physiology, 88* (2), 774–787.

Borkman, T. J. (1999). *Understanding self-help/mutual aid: Experiential learning in the commons.* New Brunswick, NJ: Rutgers University Press.

Bornstein, R. F. (1993). *The dependent personality.* New York: Guilford Press.

Borthwick, A., Holman, C., Kennard, D., McFetridge, M., Messruther, K., & Wilkes, J. (2001). The relevance of moral treatment to mental health care. *Journal of Mental Health, 10*(4), 427–439.

Bradley, K. (1995). *Who decides to do what, and when? Decision making in the clubhouse: Process and implementation.* Paper presented at the 8th International Seminar on the Clubhouse Model. Salt Lake City.

Brown, D., & Pedder, J. (1991). *Introduction to psychotherapy: An outline of psychodynamic principles and practice* (2nd ed.). London: Routledge.

Brown, W. K., & Ryan, R. M. (2004). Fostering healthy self regulation from within and without: A self-determination theory perspective. In P. A. Linley & S. Joseph (Eds.), *Positive psychology in practice* (pp. 105–119). Hoboken, NJ: John Wiley & Sons.

Brun, C., & Rapp, R. C. (2001). Strengths-based case management: Individuals' perspectives on strengths and the case manager relationship. *Social Work*, 46(3), 278–288.

Carling, P. J., & Curtis, L. C. (1992). *Review of Fountain House sponsored housing and recommendations for further development: A report to Fountain House.* Burlington, VT: Center for Community Change Through Housing and Support.

Carmichael, D. M. (1959). Community aftercare clinics and Fountain House. In M. Greenblatt and B. Simon (Eds.), *Rehabilitation of the mentally ill: Social and economic aspects.* Washington, DC: American Association for the Advancement of Sciences, Publication Vol. 58.

Carolan, M., Onaga, E., Pernice-Duca, F., & Jimenez, T. (2011). A place to be: The role of clubhouses in facilitating social support. *Psychiatric Rehabilitation Journal*, 35(2), 125–132.

Casey, E. S. (1993). *Getting back into place: Toward a renewed understanding of the place world.* Bloomington: Indiana University Press.

Chamberlin, J. (1977). *On our own: Patient-controlled alternatives to the mental health system.* New York: McGraw Hill.

———. (1987). The case for separatism. In I. L. Parker & E. Peck (Eds.), *Power in strange places* (pp. 24–26). London: Good Practices in Mental Health.

———. (1995). Rehabilitating ourselves: The psychiatric survivor movement. *International Journal of Mental Health*, 24(1), 39–46.

Chamberlin, J., Rogers, E. S., & Edison, M. L. (1996). Self-help programs: A description of their characteristics and their members. *Psychiatric Rehabilitation Journal*, 19(3), 33–42.

Chua, R. Y.-J., & Iyengar, S. S. (2006). Empowerment through choice? A critical analysis of the effects of choice in organizations. In B. M. Shaw (Ed.), *Research in organizational behavior: An annual series of analytical essays and critical reviews* (vol. 27, pp. 41–79).

Clay, S. (Ed.) (2005). *On our own, together: Peer programs for people with mental illness.* Nashville, TN: Vanderbilt University Press.

Cohen, A.P. (1985). *The symbolic construction of community.* London: Routledge.

Cook, J. A., Blyler, C. R., Leff, H. S., McFarlane, W. R., Goldberg, R. W., Donegan, K., Carey, M. A., Kaufman, C., Gold, P. B., Mueser, K. T., Shafer, M. S., Onken, S. J., & Razzano, L. A. (2008). The employment intervention demonstration program: Major findings and policy implications. *Psychiatric Rehabilitation Journal*, 38(4), 291–295.

Cooley, C. H. (1909). *Social organization: A study of the larger mind.* New York: Charles Scribner's Sons.

Corrigan, P. W., Calabrese, J. D., Diwan, S. E., Keogh, C. B., Keck, L., & Mussery, C. (2002). Some recovery processes in mutual-help groups for persons with mental illness; I: Qualitative analysis of program materials and testimonies. *Community Mental Health Journal*, *30*(4), 287–301.

Corrigan, P. W., Slopen, N. A.M., Gracia, G., Phelan, S., Keogh, C. B., & Keck, L. (2005). Some recovery processes in mutual-help groups for persons with mental illness; II: Qualitative analysis of participant interviews. *Community Mental Health Journal*, *41*(6), 721–735.

Council on Social Work Education. (2008). Educational policy and accreditation standards. Retrieved from http://www.cswe.org.

Cumming, J., & Cumming, E. (1962). *Ego and milieu: Theory and practice of environmental therapy*. Chicago: Aldine.

Davis, A. F. (1984). *Spearheads for reform: The social settlements and the progressive movement, 1890–1914*. New Brunswick, NJ: Rutgers University Press.

Deal, T. E., & Kennedy, A. A. (1982). *Corporate cultures: The rites and rituals of corporate life*. Reading, MA: Addison-Wesley.

Deci, E. L. (1995). *Why we do what we do: Understanding self-motivation*. New York: Penguin.

Deci, E. L., & Ryan, R.M. (1985). *Intrinsic motivation and self determination in human behavior*. New York: Plenum.

DeSisto, M. J., Harding, C. M., McCormick, R. V., Ashikaga, T., & Brooks, G. W. (1995a). The Maine and Vermont three-decade studies of serious mental illness: Matched comparison of cross-sectional outcome. *British Journal of Psychiatry*, *167*(3), 331–338.

———. (1995b). The Maine and Vermont three-decade studies of serious mental illness: Longitudinal course comparisons. *British Journal of Psychiatry*, *167*(3), 338–341.

Dewane, C. J. (2006). Use of self: A primer revisited. *Clinical Social Work Journal*, *34*(4), 543–558.

Dougherty, S. J. (1994). The generalist role in clubhouse organizations. *Psychosocial Rehabilitation Journal*, *18*(1), 95–108

Dougherty, S. J., Campana, K. A., Kontos, R. A., Lockhart, R., & Shaw, D. (1996). Supported education: A qualitative study of the student experience. *Psychiatric Rehabilitation Journal*, *19*(3), 59–70.

Doyle, A. (2012). Fountain House and community psychiatry. In H. L. McQuistion, W. E. Sowers, J. M. Ranz, & J. M. Feldman (Eds.), *Handbook of community psychiatry* (pp. 369–378). New York: Springer.

Drake, R. E., Becker, D. R., Clark, R. E., & Meuser, K. T. (1999). Research on the individual placement and support model of supported employment. *Psychiatric Quarterly*, *70*, 289–301.

Eddy, T. (1815). *Hints for introducing an improved mode of treating the insane in the asylum*. Speech before the governors of the New York Hospital, April 4, 1815. Governors of New York Hospital.

Ely, I. (1992). Closeness in clubhouse relationships. *Psychosocial Rehabilitation Journal, 16*(2), 62–66.

Etzioni, A. (1961). *A comparative analysis of complex organizations: On power, involvement, and their correlates.* New York: Free Press of Glencoe.

Finn, J. L., & Jacobson, M. (2008). Social justice. In T. Mizrahi & L. E. Davis, *Encyclopedia of Social Work.* (e-reference ed.). National Association of Social Workers and Oxford University Press.

Flannery, M., & Glickman, M. (1996). *Fountain House: Portraits of lives reclaimed from mental illness.* New York: Hazelden.

Freeman, T., Cameron, J. L., & McGhie, A. (1958). *Chronic schizophrenia.* New York: International University Press.

Fromm, E. (1956). *The art of loving.* New York: Harper.

Gardner, H. (1997). *Extraordinary minds: Portraits of exceptional individuals.* London: Weidenfeld & Nicolson.

Glascote, R. M., Cumming, E., Rutman, I. R., Sussex, J. N., & Glassman, S. M. (1971). *Rehabilitating the mentally ill in the community: A study of psychosocial rehabilitation centers.* Washington, DC: Joint Information Services of the American Psychiatric Association and the National Association for Mental Health.

Glazer, N. (1974). The schools of the minor professions. *Minerva, 12*(3), 346–364.

Glickman, M. (1992). What if nobody wants to make lunch?: Bottom line responsibility in the clubhouse. *Psychosocial Rehabilitation Journal, 16*(2), 55–59.

———. (2005). *The clubhouse journey to recovery.* Presentation at the 13th annual international conference on the clubhouse model, Helsinki, Finland.

Glynn, T. J. (1981). Psychological sense of community: Measurement and application. *Human Relations, 34*(9), 780–818.

Goertzel, V., Beard, J. H., & Pilnick, S. (1960). Fountain House Foundation: Case study of an ex-patient's club. *Journal of Social Issues, 16*(2), 54–61.

Grant, P. M., & Beck, A. T. (2010). Asocial beliefs as predictors of asocial behavior in schizophrenia. *Psychiatry Research, 177*(1), 65–70.

Greenblatt, M., York, R. H., & Brown, E. L. (1955). *From custodial to therapeutic patient care in mental hospitals: Explorations in social treatment.* New York: Russell Sage Foundation.

Grob, G. N. (1994). *The mad among us: A history of the care of America's mentally ill.* New York: Free Press.

Gusfield, J. R. (1975). *Community: A critical response.* New York: Harper & Row.

Hofstadter, R. (1944). *Social Darwinism in American thought, 1860–1915.* Philadelphia: University of Pennsylvania Press.

Hogan, M. F. (1994). *Recovery: The new force in mental health.* Ohio: Department of Mental Health.

Hogan, M. F., & Carling, P. J. (1992). Normal housing: A key element of a supported housing approach for people with psychiatric disabilities. *Community Mental Health Journal, 28*(3), 215–226.

Howe, M. J. A. (1990). *The origins of exceptional abilities.* Oxford: Blackwell.

Husock, H. (1992). Bringing back the settlement house. *Public Interest, 109*(Fall), 53–72.

International Center for Clubhouse Development. (2012). *2012 international clubhouse directory and resource guide.* New York: Author.

Isaac, R. J., & Armat, V. C. (1990). *Madness in the streets.* New York: Free Press.

Jackson, R. L. (2001). *The clubhouse model: Empowering applications of theory to generalist practice.* Belmont, CA: Wadsworth/Thompson Learning.

Jackson, R. L., Purnell, D., Anderson, S., & Sheafor, B. (1996). The clubhouse model for community support for adults with mental illness: An emerging opportunity for social work education. *Journal of Social Work Education, 32*(2), 172–180.

Jones, M. (1953). *The therapeutic community.* New York: Basic Books.

Jorgensen, I. S. (2004). Positive psychology: History, philosophical, and epistemological perspectives. In P. A. Linley & S. Joseph (Eds.), *Positive psychology in practice,* (pp. 15–34). Hoboken, NJ: John Wiley & Sons.

Kahn, E. (1985). Heinz, Kohut, and Carl Rogers: A timely comparison, *American Psychologist, 42*(8), 893–904.

Kauffman, C., & Scoular, A. (2004). Toward a positive psychology of executive coaching. In P. A. Linley & S. Joseph (Eds.), *Positive psychology in practice* (pp. 287–301). Hoboken, NJ: John Wiley & Sons.

Kaufman, R. (2002). What makes a great unit? *The Clubhouse Community Journal, 4,* 66–69. New York: International Center for Clubhouse Development.

Kemp, S. P., Whittaker, J. K., & Tracey, E. M. (1997). *Person-environment practice: The social ecology of interpersonal helping.* New York: Aldine de Gruyter.

Kirkpatrick, B., Fenton, W., Carpenter, W. T. J., & Marder, S. I. (2006). The NIMH-MATRICS consensus statement on negative symptoms. *Schizophrenia Bulletin, 32*(2), 214–219.

Kirst-Ashman, K. K. (2010). *Social work and social welfare: Critical thinking perspectives* (3rd ed.). Belmont, CA: Brooks/Cole, Cengage Learning.

Klein, E. (2006). In the community: Aftercare for seriously mentally ill persons from their own perspectives. In J. Rosenberg & S. Rosenberg (Eds.), *Community mental health: Challenges for the 21st century* (pp. 35–46). New York: Routledge.

Kondrat, M. E. (2008). Person-in-environment. In Terry Mizrahi & Larry E. Davis, *Encyclopedia of Social Work* (e-reference ed.). National Association of Social Workers and Oxford University Press.

REFERENCES

Kristiansen, M. (2006). *Report on a project in two Fountain House club-houses in Denmark: Project vocational method—It Makes Sense*. Copenhagen: Author.

Lamb, H. R. (1994). A century and a half of psychiatric rehabilitation in the United States. *Hospital and Community Psychiatry, 45*(10), 1015–1020.

Langer, E. (1989). *Mindfulness*. Reading, MA: Addison-Wesley.

Lanoil, J. (1976). Advocacy and social systems network: Continuity of care for the adult schizophrenic. *Psychosocial Rehabilitation Journal, 1*, 1–6.

Lehman, A. F., Kreyenbuhl, J., Buchanan, R. W., Dickerson, F. B., Dixon, L. B., Goldberg, R., Green-Paden, L. D., Tenhula, W. N., Boerescu, D., Tek, C., Sandson, N., & Steinwachs, D. M. (2004). The schizophrenia patient outcomes research team (PORT). *Schizophrenia Bulletin, 30*(2), 193–217.

Lewin, K. (1946). Action research and minority problems. *Journal of Social Issues, 2*(4), 34–46.

Lewin, R. (1992). *Complexity—Life at the edge of chaos*. New York: Macmillan.

Locke, B., Garrison, R., & Winship, J. (1998). *Generalist social work practice: Context, story, and partnership*. Stamford, CT: Cenage Learning, Inc.

Madison, E., & Maltz, B. (2012). *Community to classroom: Examination of the Fountain House supported education program*. Unpublished manuscript. New York: Fountain House.

Mancini, M. A. (2006). Consumer-providers' theories about recovery from serious psychiatric disabilities. In J. Rosenberg & S. Rosenberg (Eds.), *Community mental health: Challenges for the 21st century* (pp. 15–24). New York: Routledge.

Mancini, M. A., Hardiman, E. R., & Lawson, H. A. (2005). Making sense of it all: Consumer providers' theories about factors facilitating and impeding recovery from psychiatric disabilities. *Psychiatric Rehabilitation Journal, 29*(1), 48–55.

Manderscheid, R. W., & Henderson, M. J. (Eds.). (2001). *Mental Health, United States, 2000*. DHHS pub. no. SMA 01–3537. Rockville, MD: Center for Mental Health Services.

Mandiberg, J. M. (2000). *Strategic technology transfer in the human services: A case study of the mental health clubhouse movement and the international diffusion of the clubhouse model*. Diss., University of Michigan.

———. (2010). Another way: Enclave communities for people with mental Illness. *American Journal of Orthopsychiatry, 80*(2), 167–173.

———. (2012). The failure of social inclusion: An alternative approach through community development, *Psychiatric Services, 63*(5), 458–460.

Manoogian, S. T., & Resnick, J. S. (1976). The undermining and enhancing of intrinsic motivation. *Journal of Personality and Social Psychology, 34*(5), 915–922.

March, D., Hatch, S. L., Morgan, C., Kirkbride, J. B., Bresnahan, M., Fearon, P., & Susser, E. (2008). Psychosis and place. *Epidemiologic Reviews, 30*, 84–100.

Marwaha, S., & Johnson, S. (2004). Schizophrenia and employment: A review. *Social Psychiatry Psychiatric Epidemiology, 39*(5), 337–349.

Maslow, A. H. (1954). *Motivation and personality.* New York: Harper & Row.

McCormick, E. (December, 1957). Let's help them live again. *Readers Digest.*

McKay, C. E., Yates, B. T., & Johnsen, M. (2007). Costs of clubhouses: An international perspective. *Mental Health Services Research and Administration and Policy in Mental Health, 34*(1), 62–72.

McMillan, D. W., & Chavis, D. M. (1986). Sense of community: A definition and theory. *Journal of Community Psychology, 14*(1), 6–23.

Mechanic, D., Blider, S., & McAlpine, D. D. (2002). Employing persons with serious mental illness. *Health Affairs, 21*(5), 242–253.

Milazzo-Sayre, L. J., Henderson, M. J., Manderscheid, R. W., Bokossa, M. C., Evans, C. & Male, A. A. (2000). Persons treated in specialty mental health care programs, United States, 1997. In R. W. Manderscheid & M. J. Henderson (Eds.), *Mental health, United States, 2000.* Substance Abuse and Mental Health Services Administration, Department of Health and Human Services pub. no. SMA 01–3537. Rockville, MD: Center for Mental Health Services.

Mowbray, C., Chamberlain, P., Jennings, M., & Reed, C. (1988). Consumer-run mental health services: Results from five demonstration projects. *Community Mental Health Journal, 24*(2), 151–156.

National Association of Social Workers. (2008). *Code of Ethics* (rev. 8th ed.). Washington, DC: Author.

National Institute of Mental Health. (2008). *The number count: Mental disorders in America.* Retrieved from http://www.nimh.nih.gov/index.shtml.

Nicholls, Pauline. (2003). *Stories of hope* (video). New York: International Center for Clubhouse Development.

Norman, C. (2006). The Fountain House movement, an alternative rehabilitation model for people with mental health problems: Members' descriptions of what works. *Scandinavian Journal of Caring Sciences, 20*(2), 184–192.

Orlinsky, D. E., Grawe, K., & Parks, B. K. (1994). Process and outcome in psychotherapy: Noch einmal. In A. E. Bergin & S. L. Garfield (Eds.), *Handbook of psychotherapy and behavior change* (4th ed.) (pp. 270–376). Oxford: John Wiley & Sons.

Parks, J., Svendsen, D., Singer, P., & Foti, M. E. (2006). *Morbidity and mortality in people with serious mental illness.* Alexandria, VA: National Association of State Mental Health Program Directors (NASMHPD) Medical Directors Council.

Peckoff, J. (1992). Patienthood to personhood. *Psychosocial Rehabilitation Journal, 16* (2), 5–8.

Pernice-Duca, F., & Onaga, E. (2009). Examining the contribution of social network support to the recovery process among clubhouse members. *American Journal of Psychiatric Rehabilitation*, 12(1), 1–30.

Pinel, P. (1806). *A treatise on insanity*. Memphis: General Books.

Pistrang, N., Barker, C., & Humphreys, K. (2008). Mutual help groups for mental health problems: A review of effectiveness studies. *American Journal of Community Psychology*, 42, 110–121.

President's New Freedom Commission on Mental Health. (2002). *Interim report*. http://govinfo.library.unt.edu/mentalhealthcommission/reports/Final_Interim_Report. doc.

———. (2003). *Achieving the promise: Transforming mental health care in America*. DHHS Publication No. SMA-03–3832. Rockville, MD.

Propst, R. (1967). *Transcription from outtakes of film on Fountain House*. New York: Fountain House.

———. (1992). Standards for clubhouse programs: How and why they were developed. *Psychosocial Rehabilitation Journal*, 16(2), 25–30.

———. (1997). Stages in realizing the international diffusion of a single way of working: The clubhouse model. *New Directions for Mental Health Services*, 74, 53–66. doi: 10.1002/yd.2330227407.

Pulice, R. T., & Muccio, S. (2006). Patient, client, consumer, survivor: The mental health consumer movement in the United States. In J. Rosenberg & S. Rosenberg (Eds.), *Community mental health: Challenges for the 21st century* (pp. 7–14). New York: Rutledge.

Putnam, R. D. (2000). *Bowling alone: The collapse and revival of American community*. New York: Simon & Schuster.

Rapp, C. A., & Goscha, R. J. (2006). *The strengths model: Case management with people with psychiatric disabilities* (2nd ed.). New York: Oxford University Press.

Relph, Edward. (1976). *Place and placelessness*. London: Pion.

Reznik, L. (1987). *The nature of disease*. London: Routledge & Kegan Paul,

Rioch, D. McK., & Stanton, A. H. (1953). Milieu therapy. *Journal for the Study of Interpersonal Processes*, 16, 65–72.

Robbins, S. S. (1954). Social rehabilitation at Fountain House. *Journal of Rehabilitation*, 20 (3), 8–10, 13.

Roberts, L. J., Salem, D., Rappaport, J., Toro, P. A., Luke, D. A., & Seidman, E. (1999). Giving and receiving help: Interpersonal transactions in mutual-help meetings and psychosocial adjustment of members. *American Journal of Community Psychology*, 27(6), 841–868.

Rogers, C. R. (1961). *On becoming a person: A therapist's view of the good life*. Boston: Houghton Mifflin.

Rose, S. M. (1992). *Case management and social work practice*. White Plains, NY: Longman.

Rosenberg, J., & Rosenberg, S. (Eds.). (2006). *Community mental health: Challenges for the 21st century*. New York: Routledge.

Ryden, K. C. (1993). *Mapping the invisible landscape: Folklore, writing, and sense of place*. Iowa City: University of Iowa Press.

Sacks, O. (2009). The lost virtues of the asylum. *New York Review of Books, 56* (14).

Saleebey, D. (1992). *The strengths perspective in social work practice* (5th ed.). Boston: Pearson/Allyn & Bacon.

———. (1996). The strengths perspective in social work practice: Extensions and cautions. *Social Work, 41*(3), 296–305.

Saraceno, B. (2006). *Building awareness-reducing risks: Suicide and mental illness*. WHO Media Centre news release, http://www.who.int/mediacentre/news/releases/2006/pr53/en/index.html.

Sarason, S. B. (1974). *The psychological sense of community: Prospects for a community psychology*. San Francisco: Jossey-Bass.

Schein, E. H. (1985). *Organizational culture and leadership*. San Francisco: Jossey-Bass.

Schön, D. A. (1983). *The reflective practitioner: How professionals think in action*. New York: Basic Books.

Schonebaum, A., Boyd, J., & Dudek, K. (2006). A comparison of competitive employment outcomes for the clubhouse and PACT models. *Psychiatric Services, 57*(10), 1416–1420.

Seligman, M. E .P. (2003). Positive psychology: Fundamental assumptions. *The Psychologist, 16*(3), 126–127.

Seligman, M. E. P., & Csikszentmihalyi, M. (2000). Positive psychology: An introduction. *American Psychologist, 55*(1), 5–14.

Sheafor, B. W., & Horejsi, C. R. (2006). *Techniques and guidelines for social work practice* (7th ed.). Boston: Pearson/Allyn & Bacon.

Silverstein, S. M., & Wilkniss, S. M. (2004). At Issue: The future of cognitive rehabilitation of schizophrenia. *Schizophrenia Bulletin, 30*(4), 679–692.

Simon, B. L. (1994). *The empowerment tradition in American social work: A history*. New York: Columbia University Press.

Solomon, P. (2004). Peer support/peer provided services underlying processes, benefits, and critical ingredients. *Psychiatric Rehabilitation Journal, 34*(4), 392–401.

Sowbel, L. R., & Starnes, W. (2006). Pursuing hope and recovery: An integrated approach to psychiatric rehabilitation. In J. Rosenberg & S. Rosenberg (Eds.), *Community mental health: Challenges for the 21st century* (pp. 25–34). New York: Routledge.

Stanton, A., & Schwartz, M. (1954). *The mental hospital*. New York: Basic Books.

Stein, L. I., & Santos, A. B. (1998). *Assertive community treatment of persons with severe mental illness*. New York: W. W. Norton.

Stein, L. I., & Test, M. A. (Eds.). (1985). *The training in community living model: A decade of experience: No. 26. New directions for mental health services*. San Francisco: Jossey-Bass.

Stringer, E. T. (1999). *Action research.* Thousand Oaks, CA: Sage.

Subcommittee of the President's New Freedom Commission on Mental Health: Employment and Income Support. (February 5, 2003). *Summary report.* Washington, DC: Author.

Sullivan, H. S. (1931). Socio-psychiatric research: Its implications for the schizophrenia problem and for mental hygiene. *American Journal of Psychiatry, 10,* 977.

Susskind, L., & Cruikshank, J. (2006). *Breaking Robert's Rules: The new way to run your meeting, build consensus, and get results.* New York: Oxford University Press.

Toseland, R.W., & Rivas, R. F. (2011). *An introduction to group work practice* (7th ed.). Upper Saddle River, NJ: Pearson.

Toseland, R., & Siporin, M. (1986). When to recommend group treatment: A review of the clinical and research literature. *International Journal of Group Psychotherapy, 36*(2), 171–201.

Trout, D. L. (1980). The role of social isolation in suicide. *Suicide and Life-Threatening Behavior, 10*(1), 10–23.

Tsemberis, S. (2004a, April). Housing First, consumer choice, and harm reduction for homeless individuals with a dual diagnosis. *American Journal of Public Health, 94*(4), 651–656.

———. (2004b). "Housing first" approach. In *Encyclopedia of Homelessness,* vol. 1, 277–280. Thousand Oaks, CA: Sage.

Tsemberis, S., & Eisenberg, R. R. (2000). Pathways to housing: Supported housing for street-dwelling homeless individuals with psychiatric disabilities. *Psychiatric Service, 51*(4), 487–493.

Tuke, S., & Society of Friends. (1813). *Description of the Retreat, an institution near York for insane persons of the Society of Friends.* Reprinted by Process Press, 1996.

U.S. General Accounting Office. (1977). *Returning the mentally disabled to the community: Government needs to do more.* (HRD-76-152). Washington, DC: Author.

Velligan, D. I., & Alphs, L. D. (2008). Negative symptoms in schizophrenia: The importance of identification and treatment. *Psychiatric Times, 25*(3), 1–6.

Verhaeghe, M., Bracke, P., & Bruynooghe, K. (2008). Stigmatization and self-esteem of persons in recovery from mental illness: The role of peer support. *International Journal of Social Psychiatry, 54*(3), 206–218.

Vorspan, R. (2000). Clubhouse relationships need work! *Clubhouse Community Journal, 2,* 33–36. New York: International Center for Clubhouse Development.

———. (2004). Member role/staff role: Another look. *Clubhouse Community Journal, 5,* 25–29. New York: International Center for Clubhouse Development.

Vygotsky, L. S. (1978). *Mind in society.* Cambridge, MA: Harvard University Press.

Waegemakers Schiff, J., Colman, H., & Miner, D. (2008). Voluntary participation in rehabilitation: Lessons learned from a clubhouse environment. *Canadian Journal of Community Mental Health*, 27(1), 65–78.

Waters, B. (1992). The work unit: The heart of the clubhouse. *Psychosocial Rehabilitation Journal*, 16(2), 41–48.

Wender, L. (1936). The dynamics of group psychotherapy and its application. *Journal of Nervous and Mental Disorders*, 84, 54–60.

Whitaker, D. (1975). Some conditions for effective work with groups. *British Journal of Social Work*, 5, 423–439.

Whitley, R., & Drake, R. E. (2010). Recovery: A dimensional approach. *Psychiatric Services*, 61(12), 1248–1250.

Whitley, R., Harris, M., Fallot, R. D., & Berley, R. W. (2007). The active ingredients of intentional recovery communities: Focus group evaluation. *Journal of Mental Health*, 17(2), 173–182.

Whitley, R., Strickler, D., & Drake, R. E. (2011). Recovery centers for people with severe mental illness: A survey of programs. *Community Mental Health Journal*. DOI: 10.1007/s10597-011-9427-4.

Whiteley, S. (2004). The evolution of the therapeutic community. *Psychiatric Quarterly*, 75(3), 233–248.

Wills, T. A. (1991). Social support and interpersonal relationships. In M. S. Clarke (Ed.), *Prosocial behavior* (pp. 265–289). Newbury Park, CA: Sage.

Wolf, J. M. (1958). *Report on certain aspects of an extended program*. Report to the Board of Directors. New York: Fountain House Foundation.

Wolfensberger, W. (1972). *Principle of normalization in human services*. Toronto: Canadian Association for the Mentally Retarded.

Wolfensberger, W., & Tillman, S. (1982). A brief outline of the principle of normalization. *Rehabilitation Psychology*, 27(3), 131–145.

INDEX

acceptance, basic, 118
achievement, recognition of, 99
activity group therapy (AGT), xxv, xxvii, 3–4, 20–22, 27, 157; choice in, 19; diagnosis in, 14; groups in, 17–20; implementation of, 6; and medical personnel, 15–16; methodological design of, 7; modeling behavior of therapist in, 18, 19; and need to be needed, 51; new relational approach in, 14–17; patient participation, 33; and patient pathology, 16; practice tenets of, 20, 21; relationships in, 13–14; and resurgence of humane psychiatric treatment, 8–14; and social practice, 75; strengths approach in, xvii, 14, 16–17; task-oriented group work of, 20; time away from hospital in, 19; treatment design, 4–8, 7
advocacy, community support as, 103–104
agreement, in consensus decision making, 83

American Psychiatric Association (APA), xix
Anderson, Stephen B., xxi, 28, 32, 36, 151, 152, 161n5
Anthony, W. A., 109
Assertive Community Treatment (ACT), xxiv, xxv
asylum: 19th century innovation of, xvi, 9–10; and working community, 145
autonomy, 55–56, 57. 126–129
avoidance, in patient under treatment, 110

Bandura, Albert, xxv, 86, 87, 89, 90, 91, 92, 94, 98, 99, 100, 102, 106, 116, 121, 122
basic skills, in transitional employment, 37
Beard, John Henderson, xiii, xxii–xxv, 2, 22, 43, 144; and AGT, 18; arrival at Fountain House, 27–29; death of, 156; on field assignment, xxvii, 3; on functioning of Fountain House, 69, 70; on helping act,